Sex, Drugs, Etc., Etc., Etc.

SEX, DRUGS, ETC., ETC., ETC.

Unforgettable Lessons that will Change the Lives
of Teenagers and Twenty-Somethings

ROB SHINDLER J.D.
ILLUSTRATED BY JOE CHOUINARD

MASCOT BOOKS

www.mascotbooks.com

For more information, please contact:
Mascot Books
620 Herndon Parkway, Suite 320
Herndon, VA 20170
info@mascotbooks.com

Library of Congress Control Number: 2021908869

CPSIA Code: PRV0721A
ISBN-13: 978-1-64543-743-7

Printed in the United States

To Isabella, Oliver, and Sage.
Being a lawyer gives me a living. Being your
dad gives me a life.

And to Anz.
July 8, 1985, is the day my world began.
Everything I am, I am because of you, and
every moment we spend together, I spend in a
state of flow.

"It's easier to build strong children
than to repair broken men [and women]."

Frederick Douglass

INTRODUCTION

Sex, drugs, and rock 'n' roll.

Originally, this phrase was used to describe the lifestyles of rock stars—like the Beatles, Elvis, and the Rolling Stones. Fast cars, fast girls, fast guys. Fireworks every day of the year—twice on the Fourth of July. In reality, these words better represent *your* world. Generation Z has it way harder today than any other before you.

So much pressure, so many seductions. Facebook, Instagram, Twitter, Snapchat, TikTok.

Swiping, swooping, swapping. Everybody knowing where you are and what you're eating 24/7. It is like living inside a volcano running a billion degrees at all times. The outside world watching through a microscope, judging all your moves with intense scrutiny.

There are so many books and educational tools out there dedicated to bombarding you with information on how you should act and think, helping you safely maneuver from middle school to high school to college and, ultimately, into the real world.

There are playbooks on how to enter adulthood. Tips to score in the top 1 percent on your SAT. Blueprints on getting into that elite university. Guidelines for picking the perfect prom dress.

One publication actually labels Gen Z the dumbest generation of all generations. In 2016, *Collins English Dictionary* officially added the term *snowflake generation* to their latest edition, defining Gen Z as less resilient and more prone to taking offense than any other generation in history. This assertion cannot be further from the truth. I believe you're the smartest and the bravest; you're the ones who will change our world.

But what if you're arrested for having drugs in your car? What if you have sex with the wrong person? What if you find yourself in a stormy situation without an umbrella? Felons don't get front row seats at Harvard.

Try DM'ing wearing handcuffs. Writing the perfect resume from a jail cell won't help you land your dream job.

That's why I wrote this book—to give you a map that will help you stay on course, and if you should slip, it will show you how to catch yourself.

THE STAR OF OUR SHOW

As I said in the introduction, one publication crowns you the dumbest generation of all generations. This is why I chose a very special guest to serve as the spokesperson and temporary legal expert during our journey together throughout this book. So without further ado, allow me to introduce you to Dumbo the Octopus.

"Hey everybody. Nice to meet you. Yes, I'm real! Although I am anything but dumb. My fins look like huge ears, just like the famous flying elephant from the Disney movies. That's how I actually got my name, Dumbo. *National Geographic* says I'm one of the most adorable creatures they have ever seen. I have to humbly agree. I have three hearts. And although I may be smaller compared to other octopuses, I am fast and strong and a survivor—much like you. I am capable of hanging out at depths so deep in the ocean, predators are rarely able to find me. I'm kind of a superhero. I also try to be funny; I'm kind of like the class clown. But the stuff we'll be discussing together is no joke. Please know if it ever seems like I'm lecturing or trying to scare you with some of our stories, that's never my intention. Education is power, and I'm just trying to talk about some important issues together to help make sure you have choices and stay safe. Thanks for listening. Now, let's dive in!"

SEX

Peekaboo, I See You!

In a million years, when a person wants to know what some teenagers' and young adults' lives looked like back in 2020, someone should hand them a shovel, have them dig up a time capsule, put some batteries in the remote control, and let them watch an episode of *Euphoria*.

For those who have never seen *Euphoria*, it's HBO's teen drama starring Zendaya, who plays Rue, an out-of-control drug addict just out of rehab. Her best friend is Jules, a transgender girl trying to discover her place in the world. It also features Nate, the school's star quarterback who is dealing with his own sexual issues. Like a horrible car accident, you can't possibly tear your eyes away from the television screen. Had I known this is what secondary education looks like, I would have probably homeschooled my three kids and only allowed them outside the house one hour a day for air and jumping jacks.

You have already heard a billion times how posting naked photos and videos can follow you around forever, preventing you from getting into certain colleges or being hired for that dream job. So, I won't waste your time repeating those warnings. Cassie, the popular cheerleader in the show, has heard 'em all before, and she's sick of them, too.

In the episode "Stuntin' Like My Daddy," Cassie's having real problems navigating her many relationships as lots of rumors about her sexual history fly around the school. She is lecturing her single mom, Suzie, on how Suzie and other adults don't understand that today's teenagers are simply expressing themselves by putting naked videos on the Internet—this is what everyone does—it's their body and their choice. Besides, it's no big deal. Or is it?

Hammerin' Hank

A high school baseball team traveled out of state for a big tournament. The chaperones were the head coach, the assistant principal, and the school's chaplain.

What can possibly go wrong here, right?

One of the players, Henry, hooked up with a sixteen-year-old girl he met at a party. They had sex in his hotel room. Without her knowing, Henry, who was also sixteen years old, recorded the whole thing on video. Then he shared it with his teammates ... then with the rest of the world by posting it on his Facebook page and uploading the video on YouTube. As the team's bus headed home, the girl discovered she was a star. The post already had over 1,800 hits.

A few days later, Henry was arrested and charged as an adult with felony child pornography. If convicted, he could not only go to jail, but under the guidelines of the law, he would have a permanent criminal record and be forced to register as a sex offender.

You might be wondering, *Wait a second! Didn't Cassie the cheerleader just tell her mom, it's "our body, our choice." Besides, both kids are under eighteen years old. Someone sixteen years old, a child himself, can't possibly be charged with distributing child pornography over the Internet, can he?*

Dumbo, any words of wisdom?

"Well, unfortunately they can. According to Wallin & Klarich, a powerful team of defense attorneys specializing in these type of cases, 'in order for the prosecution to convict you of possession of child pornography, you must knowingly possess or share something that shows a person under the age of eighteen engaging in some form of sexual conduct or activity. If both people involved are under the age of eighteen, they could both face a felony.' In our case, since Henry knew about the recording, but the girl he slept with didn't, he's the only one charged. And even though Henry's just sixteen years old himself, he can still be tried in court as an adult.

Rob Shindler

You're young; it's exciting. Living in the moment and being invincible. I get it! And it's true, they are your bodies, and it is your decision. However, education is power. So, before pressing the Post button, just know the possible risks so you can protect yourselves."

Sweet Sixteen

Kevin was raised to be a real gentleman, just like one of those actors from the olden days your great-grandparents watched in black-and-white films. Holding doors open. Pulling out chairs. Going to get the car in the rain for his date. Kind and considerate. Just a really great guy.

When Becky started dating him, her parents were thrilled. *What a nice young man,* they both thought. He had two jobs. He was starting college in the fall after delaying it for a year to save up for tuition. He came into the house with a strong handshake, looking everyone in the eye. He seemed so mature for being nineteen years old. What a sweet gesture it was from him bringing Becky's mom fresh lilies to their family's Fourth of July picnic. It was all going so wonderful. Until it wasn't.

You see, Becky was nearly four years younger than Kevin. She turned sixteen a few weeks before. She was an honor student and a shining star in her own right. She was daddy's little girl. So when Becky and Kevin's romance came tumbling down at the end of the summer, a real-life *Romeo and Juliet* tragedy began.

There was no disputing the fact that the baby was Kevin's. Both of them were virgins—or at least, they *had* been. Kevin received a call on Monday morning. The detective's voicemail asked him to come down to the station to discuss the situation. *What situation?* He and Becky had pledged to remain good friends even after their breakup. However, her dad had other plans. After all, that was his daughter that Kevin got pregnant. Becky's dad was the one who contacted the police.

Kevin's freshman year of college was quickly put on pause. It was difficult to make it to his first literature class on the suburban campus because he was set to appear at the courthouse downtown for his arraignment that same day. He was eventually charged with two counts of criminal sexual assault, also known as *statutory rape*. Statutory rape is indefensible under the law. Although some states may look at these underage relationships slightly differently based on how many years separate the couple or how young the minor actually is, the overwhelming majority rules in the same way—a person under the age of eighteen cannot legally give their consent. It doesn't matter that they were in love and both wanted to have sex. Or that initially Becky's parents loved Kevin and approved of their dating. Or that Kevin held open doors, pulled out chairs, or ran in the rain to get the car. Regardless of any of this, the fact that Becky was only sixteen years old at the time of their relationship means that she couldn't give her consent. Even if she had technically said it was okay. Therefore, the intercourse was considered nonconsensual, and Kevin plead guilty. Zero tolerance. (You'll be hearing these

Rob Shindler

two words a lot.) It's like Kevin now has two different identities. "That" guy and "this" guy.

He had no prior criminal history; he never even got a parking ticket. Therefore, Kevin was sentenced to two years probation and a felony conviction, which is permanent. So much for the dream of someday becoming a lawyer himself. However, this was the least of his problems. The legislature makes it a mandatory requirement that in almost every type of sex offender case, the person convicted must register with their state as a sex offender. This means Kevin cannot live within 500 feet of a church, school, park, playground, day care center, or several other types of establishments. He had to move out of his family's house where he grew up because it was across the street from a park where kids play.

You might be thinking, *Hold on. Where's he supposed to go? He's only eighteen years old. He can't afford his own apartment. Can he move in with his aunt and uncle?*

Let's ask someone who knows a thing or two about having two different identities. Well, Super D, can he?

"Unfortunately, he can't, because they live too close to a school."

How about his older brother's place?

"Too close to a church."

What about his best friend's house?

"Not sure. Some families may be uncomfortable with a convicted sex offender living in their home. Also, you know how there are those lists floating around neighborhoods *where people whisper, 'Did you know so-and-so down the block is a . . .' Well, Kevin is now on those lists. And hopefully his parents can get their money back for the new computer they bought him for graduation, because under the law, in many jurisdictions a registered sex offender cannot access the Internet or even have an iPhone."*

Well, at least when his two years of probation are up, his name gets wiped off the list, right?

"He's registered as a sex offender forever. You don't need to have X-ray vision to see his life is forever changed."

What about his two jobs?

"Unfortunately, he lost one right after they found out about this. He's on the hunt for another gig to help him pay the child support he's now going to be responsible for during the next eighteen years of his new child's life."

Is Kevin really a criminal? We could agree to disagree on the answer. I have my own opinion. Certainly, the facts of his situation are different from the horrible cases we normally read about in the newspaper and watch on television. However, society is too busy these days to take the time to read the fine print. Nobody will ever search the reports to see the specific circumstances behind the charges. Simply stated, under the law, he's now just another convicted sex offender, and that's all anyone will see. No fresh lilies will ever take that stink away.

We don't choose who we fall in love with or when we fall. Under different circumstances, Kevin and Becky could have someday gotten married and had a family together under less stressful circumstances. And even though it's true that some states look at these situations differently than others, the legal waters are just too murky to swim blindly in. Our hearts should never need to be guided by age—but sometimes they do.

Free Willy

Kevin knew Becky was underage and still had sex with her. But what if he didn't know? What if he thought she was of age? What if she "looked" of age? Would this make a difference?

That's a whale of a question, right?

William was valedictorian of his class. So when the principal from his old high school asked him to come home from his junior year of college for the weekend to speak at an awards assembly, it was a no-brainer for him. Will was a big deal back then, and everyone was really excited for his return. Especially Amanda.

Mandy's cousin was tight with Will, and she had heard all the stories, including the one when he broke the basketball conference record by scoring thirty-eight points in one game. Mandy was the hottest girl in her class. Her freshmen class. She was fifteen years old . . . but looked twenty-five.

However, when they met after the assembly in the parking lot, Mandy told Will how excited she was to start at U of M the next year. She told him she knew exactly what sorority she was pledging, how she already had her roommate picked out, and how she already decided to major in journalism. She shared all her dreams and hopes in his car on their drive home.

Does Will know Mandy's fifteen years old?

No.

Does he know she's under eighteen?

No.

Does it matter?

Unfortunately, no.

After having sex in the backseat of his Mustang, they stopped for an Italian ice, and then Will dropped her off at her house. That night, Mandy posted a selfie of the two of them kissing goodbye. Then, she told her best friend all about what happened . . . who then told her mom. The following morning, the shit hit the fan. Will could be seen crying in his mugshot.

Once again, these criminal charges are also indefensible. Zero tolerance. It simply doesn't matter how old Mandy looked, what she was wearing, or what she did or did not say. The test often applied by a court in making determinations is: did the older party know or SHOULD they have known that the other person was underage? Again, the legal waters in these situations are murky. And even though different judges can make different decisions, you just need to be cautious when making yours.

I know you can't exactly ask for someone's birth certificate, but before getting in the backseat of that Mustang, please try to know the other person's age. It's really important to your future and theirs.

Dancing the Night Away

Sometimes, certain situations hit so close to home, you feel their effects inside your bones. That's what happened to me when I heard about Roxanne. Although we've never met, all I want to do is hug her mom and dad and never let go, promising that every little thing is gonna be all right.

Roxanne and her friends were high school seniors who lived in the city. At the beginning of the school year, they all ordered their own fake IDs. It's amazing what you can get these days for eighty-five dollars. You couldn't even tell they were fake. There was a reflection when you held it up to the light. There was a hologram of the state seal. It was like it was created by van Gogh. They heard about this new club that just opened in the suburbs. The place made their own vodka. Roxie wasn't a huge drinker, but she loved to dance. She and her friends used to stay up until dawn creating different TikTok videos together. They were so good.

Driving to work every morning, I pass by this daycare center where I'm mesmerized by a long line of adorable toddlers literally linked by an elastic walking rope as they wobble together toward the playground. This nylon apparatus connects child to child to child, making it less difficult for the teachers to keep tabs on each preschooler.

If only we had a concoction like this for teenagers hanging out after the carriage turns into a pumpkin.

It was 2:00 a.m., and Roxie was exhausted. Her feet were swollen. She told the four other girls she called an Uber and would text them when she got home. They found her phone in a bush outside the Dunkin' Donuts across the street from the club. As Roxie waited for her ride alone outside, a man grabbed her, threw her in his car, and drove off. The rape lasted a little more than eight minutes.

"One of my all-time favorite quotes from SpongeBob Squarepants is 'F for friends who do stuff together . . .'

Hey, Roxie's friends. Not to be rude, but what the heck were you all thinking?

Rule one. Never let a friend leave a bar or a party alone.

Rule two. You never get a re-do if you forget rule one.

You go together, you come back together. No exceptions."

Sin City

Shana and her sorority sisters were in Las Vegas celebrating the end of their semester. This was a rite of passage for many college juniors around the country. Every May, thousands of twenty-somethings from universities near and far gather together for three days and three nights inside the City That Never Sleeps. What happens in Vegas, stays in Vegas. Until now. This incident needs to be shared with every sister, brother, daughter, son, cousin, friend, stranger . . . you know.

After seeing one of those extravagant Cirque du Soleil shows—you know, the kind that makes the person sitting next to you say, "Holy shit, how do they do that?"—everyone made plans to meet up at a rooftop dance club. One of the girl's dads knew a guy who knew a guy who knew the bouncer at the door. There was a special table reserved in the back area waiting for them with all the bells and whistles, including bottle service. For those not familiar, bottle service is where you get to look super-duper important and pay $225 for a bottle of vodka that normally costs $24.95.

Shana had already downed four Tito's and tonics during the show and decided to skip the club to head back to the hotel where they were staying. However, unlike Roxie, she didn't tell her friends she was leaving; she was planning on just texting them from the cab. After informing Carl the Uber driver where she wanted to go, she noticed her phone was dead. She asked Carl if she could borrow his charger, which is all Carl need-ed to know.

Their first stop was a few miles away at a Chase ATM where Carl held Shana at gunpoint and forced her to withdraw $1,000. Then they vanished off the grid. The strip in Las Vegas is known for its ginormous hotels and casinos. It's only about 4.2 miles long, but if you drive northeast on Interstate 15 for about fifty-five minutes, you'll end up smack in the middle of Valley of Fire State Park, which is the desert. However, Carl did not have his sights set on taking a beautiful hike through a canyon.

When the other girls woke up the next morning, Shana was not in her bed. She was nowhere to be found. The entire fourteenth floor of the Bellagio became frantic. Eventually, a family in a motor home saw Shana walking and gave her a ride back into town. Apparently after driving to the desert, Carl lit a roaring fire and spent a few hours frightening the crapola out of Shana with his crazy eyes and scary stories. Then he just left her there. According to Shana, nothing else happened, and she refused to go to the hospital or seek any medical attention.

"Hey, I spend most of my time eating worms on the bottom of the sea, so what do I know? I get sometimes friends get separated. Always let each other know when you're leaving, and if possible, always check your phone battery and carry a portable charger with you."

I Got My Eyes on You. All 29,000,000 of Them.

The Dad of the Decade trophy with my name etched into it may be arriving a little late this year, because unlike some parents, I don't get upset when we're at a restaurant and my three kids are on their phones. I'm just grateful they still want to have dinner together.

According to a recent research study, one in three teenagers sends or receives over one hundred text messages a day. So what?

I'm an old fart, and I text until my fingers hurt. It's not developing a case of rigor mortis from over texting that will get you into trouble. It's what you are sending and how often you are sending it that can put you in a lawyer's waiting room. Here's a good rule: assume every single person living in the state of Texas is reading your text. That's 29,000,000 people. Try not to put a word, thought, or photo on the Internet you would not want one of those 29,000,000 pairs of eyeballs seeing.

Education is Power with a capital P. You can get so much of it off the Internet. It's not breaking screen time records on your laptop that can cause you problems, it's what you are searching for that can sometimes get you into trouble. Think about those same 29,000,000 people all scrunched together inside the back of your computer eyeballing exactly what buttons you are pressing on your keyboard.

Buddy and Jack were just fooling around on Buddy's dad's computer when one of them typed in the search bar: "Teenaged Naked Young Girls." Suddenly, up popped thousands and thousands of images. Although the exact ages weren't specifically listed, they could certainly tell most of the photos are of really younger girls, many of whom were clearly still in primary school.

A few months later, Mr. Olsen, Buddy's dad, brought his Apple Computer into Best Buy to have it serviced by the Geek Squad for some technical issues he was experiencing. The following Wednesday, the neighbors all came out of their houses to watch as the FBI banged on the Olsens' front door with a search warrant.

Mr. Olsen didn't use his computer to look up anything illegal. Some of you might be wondering if he can still be charged with child pornography. Want to weigh in on this one, Dumbo?

"Yup."

To some, this might not seem fair.

"I agree, but it's his computer in his possession. And since he's a loyal, loving dad, he'd never throw his son under the bus. He took the blame himself. The problem with child pornography is it's also one of those offenses that can have long-lasting effects if you're found guilty. Depending on the specific facts, it may or may not lead to jail time. But like Henry, Kevin, and Will, there's always the possibility of facing a permanent felony conviction, which will stay on your record forever; just as with the others, there is also the requirement of registering as a sex offender."

Does the law say how many photos are needed to cause you a problem?

"Technically, one's enough. The more photos, of course, the worse the potential charges."

What if the girls on the screen look older than they really are?

"I know you're probably getting sick of these two words, but . . . Zero Tolerance. Playing around on the computer is fun. I myself spend hours on it checking out new recipes and places to travel. You just have to be careful and remember: When you're watching something, someone could be watching you."

New Orleans is an awesome place. It's like going to Disneyland, a concert, and Mars all at once. Voted greatest weekend getaway by *Condé Nast Traveler* magazine, it's also the wonderful home to an amazing college—Tulane University. Some of

the brightest minds in the country end up in the Big Easy.

The roommates on Broadway Street had lived together since freshman year. They were a perfect blend of smarts and beauty. They always had each others' backs. One night, they decided to blow off Bourbon Street and stay in for a quiet night of *The Bachelorette* and sushi . . . and red wine. Lots of red wine. The next thing you know, the four musketeers were dueling it out in a dance contest. Jumping up and down on the beds having a good old-fashioned pillow fight like they were back at a seventh-grade sleepover.

Then, the gloves came off. Actually, the tops. Suddenly, they were all naked from the waist up. And then Gabby started snapping pictures with her new iPhone X. "Smile for the birdie!" she giggled.

Later that night, she sent the photos to her twin sister, Annabella, who was studying accounting at University of Alabama. At least, Gabby *thought* she was sending it to just her. Bella may have been excellent with numbers. Gabby, not so much. She accidentally sent the pics to her family group text, which consisted of twenty-two different relatives, including, but not limited to, Nanna Doe Doe, GaMa Zelda, Grandpa George, and last but not least, ninety-four-year-old Aunt Gertie, who nearly keeled over and died when she saw the eight topless girls in high definition on her phone screen. Thank God little ten-year-old cousin Ricky with mild intermittent asthma had his cell turned off, or he could have blown a gasket!

"I remember what it's like to be young. I may not look it, but I had quite the bod back in the day. You should have seen me in a bikini. Just try to make sure when you're sharing photos, they're going exactly where you want them to go. You don't need little Ricky having that as the screen saver on his phone."

Tastes Just Like Chicken . . . Sort Of

Swipe right, swipe left. Everyone's doing it, including Violet.

You know how most kids go through that awkward stage for a brief period of time? Acne, weight issues, voice changing. For me, this period lasted from age ten to twenty-three. Some people have bad hair days. I had a bad hair decade. If there were dating apps back when I was your age, my guess is I would have been nicknamed Casper the Friendly Ghosted.

Violet met Nick on Tinder and swiped right. They hit it off from the first message. On the third date, she knew she wanted a fourth. And a fifth. For the fifth date, he invited her to his apartment for a home-cooked meal. It was so cute how he bragged about his special spaghetti Bolognese. A recipe passed down from his great grandmother from Sicily with a very secret ingredient he can't divulge. There was a little stutter in his speech she found really endearing. Maybe they would go wine tasting in the summer.

Halfway into the meal, Vi began to have intense stomach discomfort. The pain was almost unbearable. Like a space alien was trying to exorcise itself from her belly button. Mr. Secret Sauce offered to have her lay down on his couch. She declined; she'd rather go home. He asked her again, but Violet had already called an Uber.

Back home, the pain got worse. She was crumpled in a ball on the floor of her parents' bedroom. Violet's mom eased her into the station wagon and slowly drove to the hospital. After an abdominal X-ray, the ER doctor joined by a uniformed police officer entered her hospital room.

"Where did you eat tonight? Who were you with? Did your date happen to have a birthmark on his left cheek about the size of a dime?" the police officer asked.

He did.

Turns out, the secret ingredient is human flesh. You heard me. *Human freaking flesh.* Only a few days old. According to the officer, the apartment where Nick was staying was an Airbnb that was rented by the night. The spookiest part of it all—as if we need any more spooky—this was not the first time the guy had done this. There had been similar reports from other girls around the area.

"I know what you're going to say. The chances of this kind of thing happening are one in a million. You're right. I also know even after hearing this story, few of you will close the book on your dating apps, and you shouldn't. It's how people meet each other. I get it. Just be careful. Do your homework. We spend more time investigating our Uber driver's rating and researching the best place to get a burrito at 4:30 a.m. than we do on who we are dating. Ask questions that need to be asked. Investigate. And remember, sometimes ordering a pizza is the better way to go."

Teddy Bear

When someone turns the location searching on their computer into action, futures can be derailed. I wish someone could have talked with Donny before his life would be changed forever.

Donny was twenty-one years old and had recently dropped out of college with just a semester to go. He moved back in with his parents and had been spending a lot of time in their basement drinking, playing video games, and trying to rediscover himself.

Donny's sister ordered off Amazon—a lot. The delivery driver even knew her shoe size and favorite color. All the empty cardboard boxes were stored in the basement until trash day came. At night when he couldn't sleep, Donny often grabbed a lighter off the end table and started lighting the corner strips of the boxes on fire. He always blew out the flames right before they caused any real damage.

Donny logged lots of time on his laptop. His favorite site was a chat room dedicated to younger audiences fourteen years old and below.

He started having conversations with a twelve year old. They started talking about what he wanted to do to her and what she wanted to do to him. These discussions were pretty graphic. **Strike One.**

A few days later, she sent him photos of her private parts, and in return, he sent photos of his.
Strike Two.

A week later, they agreed to meet in the parking lot of the Jewel-Osco on Cosgrove Avenue. He said he'd be wearing the grey hooded sweatshirt with a picture of Clifford the Big Red Dog on the front.
Strike Three.

Talking with an underage girl on the computer about sex can get you arrested.

The naked photos are an automatic felony.

Intending to meet her in your car outside the grocery store holding a stuffed teddy bear after telling her how much you can't wait to have sex with her in the motel . . . bring your toothbrush, Donny—you're sleeping in jail.

When he arrived to the parking lot, the police officers swarmed him.

Forgive my language, but you don't need to screw to be screwed.

9-1-1. I need some backup here. Anybody in the area?

"I'm a firefighter, not a doctor, but I'll try to help. It seems to me that Donny has some burning issues that need to be addressed. Deep down, he knows a twenty-one-year-old man should not be hanging out in chat rooms trying to hook up with twelve-year-old girls. Before doing things you know are questionable, ask yourself this question: Would I want anyone else in the world to know what I'm about to do? If the answer is no, it's probably something you should not do.

"We all have our own issues. You think it's easy getting this helmet over these ears? Some of us drink too much. Some of us smoke too much. Some of us have siblings who shop online too much. Having a problem is nothing to be embarrassed about. Having a problem and not doing something about it, that's on us.

"So here's some free advice. Get some! Talk to someone— someone who can help. A parent, a therapist, or even a lawyer . . . before you get online and definitely before getting behind the wheel to go meet a sixth grader in a grocery store parking lot. Getting help afterward will be too late."

Ever since she was small, our daughter Isabella wanted to be all grown up. When she came out in the delivery room, she was looking for the car keys. I remember her prancing around the house in my wife's dress, stumbling down the stairs in high heels and covered  from head to toe with every piece of jewelry she could reach in our closet. I'd constantly tell her, "Just be a little girl for as long as you can—this adulthood stuff can be Trouble with a capital T."

In third grade, she knew exactly where she wanted to go to high school—Walter Payton College Prep—because the building was named after her daddy's favorite Chicago Bears football player. In sixth grade, she officially "committed" to Duke University—she thought one of the basketball players was really cute. In reality, like a lot of teens, she had no clue where she wanted to study. She just knew she wanted to get there as quickly as possible. Sometimes we land right where we're supposed to. Sometimes, it's *kaboom*.

College campuses are overflowing with temporary stupidity. Not in classrooms, but in the dorms. And the quads. And in fraternity and sorority houses. And on the streets and inside bars. And over telephones and under blankets. This temporary stupidity is changing the courses of lives. As Jackie Winfield wrote in an online article from The International Child and Youth Care Network back in 2006, "Stupidity has great value . . .

there is growth and learning in stupidity . . . it's a great teacher, not always a kind one, but an effective one."

It was Orientation Week, and Jane had put the finishing touches on her dorm room. It wasn't exactly home, but she had to admit, it felt really homey. Even Jeff, her stuffed animal hippo, seemed to be smiling. It was time to celebrate.

There was a notice stapled to the wall in the lobby inviting all incoming freshmen to a meet and greet at the Shoe, a popular hangout on Clover Avenue. Jane hadn't eaten all day. Once the Jäger bombs started, they never stopped.

When she woke up in her bed, she had no recollection of getting back to her floor or who the naked guy next to her was. It was the same schedule for the next week. Just like a California wildfire, word spread about the crazy girl in 2H. She even earned a nickname—Jäger Jane.

The night before classes began, Jane was taken to the local hospital after passing out in the boys' bathroom. Upon being discharged, she was transported by campus police to the town's drunk tank, which is a twenty-four-hour jail cell for people who were excessively intoxicated.

Jane's school happened to be in a state where public intoxication was a crime that goes on your record. A first offense was usually a simple misdemeanor resulting in arrest, a maximum fine of $625, and thirty days in jail. A simple misdemeanor wouldn't jeopardize Jane's dream of becoming a veterinarian. The remainder of her semester, though, could be at risk.

The following morning, she was summoned to the dean's office. She was ordered to see the school's psychologist twice a week to monitor her binge drinking issues. She also had to write a five-hundred-word essay on the risks of abusing alcohol, and she was put on probation for two months. After successfully completing her probation and getting her life back on track, eventually Jane ended up making the dean's list for several semesters in a row and soared to great heights of personal success.

Despite this, a few of the players on the lacrosse team had shirts made to keep her reputation alive and well. On the front of the shirt was a picture of Tarzan with the words "Me Tarzan." On the back was a photo of Jane passed out next to the toilet clutching a bottle with the words "Me Jäger."

"Look, you're in college. Lots of you at some point will probably have a few of those kind of nights. We all have. The key is to listen for the game show buzzer in your head. You'll know when you hear it because when it goes off, you will know exactly what to do. And what not do. More about the buzzer in chapter two."

Pick Me, Pick Me, Pick Me.

A few miles from Jane, rush week was roaring strong at the most popular fraternity on Greek Row. There were kegs as far as the eyes could glaze. Both Todd's older brother and his dad were Lambdas. He just had to get in.

On the first night of bid week, one of the fifth-year seniors gave

Todd a nickname that would stick with him throughout his four years.

T-bag. Todd was treasurer of his high school class, so when he accidentally walked into the room filled with an army of bodies, he quickly counted nine upperclassmen dudes and one freshman girl. She was being passed around. Todd froze. He was a mannequin watching the unthinkable.

Consent is defined as "giving permission for something to happen." Nobody should be okay with what was going down in that room.

"Shut the *bleep bleep bleep*'n door before I kick your ass, T-bag," one of the upperclassmen screamed. Like a good soldier, that was exactly what Todd did. He sat in the corner and watched. There's no way Todd was happy about being in that room. And not to excuse his inaction, but many people in similar situations also become paralyzed with fear and feel unable to step out from the quicksand of silence. But in these situations, we need to find the lion within ourselves and roar on behalf of the vulnerable.

It took a few months for justice. However, once it arrived, it descended quickly. Everyone was arrested, including Todd. Rape in the second degree. Failing to act can be as dangerous as the act itself. Sexual assault convictions can carry jail sentences between three to thirty years.

"Silence is sometimes not golden. Sometimes other people can only be heard through your voice."

You can't wait to get to college. And now, you can't wait to leave. In 1923, a professor at the University of Delaware created the very first college study abroad program. See the world and have your loved ones pay for it!

According to IndiaToday.in out of New Delhi, there are many benefits of studying abroad, as the experience has a great impact on an individual's life. Moreover, you get to see different places, and you get to know different people with different beliefs that broaden your thinking.

Fast forward to September 2019. Francesca was so excited to visit the birthplace of her great grandparents—Italy. Frankie closed her eyes, kept them closed for a few seconds, then slowly opened them up just to make sure it was all really real. She finally made it. Since fourth grade, she had dreamt of this moment. Aunt Theresa's postcards from when she was a little girl didn't do the view justice. Maybe after graduation she could come back to study Leonardo da Vinci, Michelangelo, and other famous artists.

After the nine-hour flight and spending two more hours singing and laughing together on the bus ride to their hotel, the girls became best friends before even stepping into the lobby. After dropping her luggage in her room, Frankie met the others downstairs in the foyer. Onto a night of fun.

Francesca was asleep in the bathtub filled with ice when she was awoken by a chambermaid who didn't speak English. She just pointed down for Frankie to read the note left on her thigh.

"Get to the emergency room as soon as you can." It was scribbled in pencil.

She felt dizzy and swollen. Then she saw it. Like laces on an old football, she was stitched from the top of her breast bone to the side of her belly button just below the ribs. She was suddenly reminded of the scar on Frankenstein's forehead in those horror films she watched with her dad late at night on the sofa.

A local doctor was called by security, and in broken English he compassionately explained to Frankie, "Somebody drugged you and stole one of your kidneys."

Nine words you never think of hearing. But that's exactly what happened. Francesca drank too much, had a date rape tablet dropped in her drink, and got her kidney taken out in the bathtub of her hotel room.

A beautiful twenty-year-old woman chose to study abroad during the second semester of her junior year. She kissed her mom and stepdad goodbye and hugged her twin sister outside the Lufthansa terminal. Courtney, her sister, decided to remain back in the States. They exchanged pillows before leaving for the airport just so they'd still somehow feel connected. And six days later, they only had three kidneys between them.

"I know, I know. You don't believe it. Nobody gets their kidney stolen. And who eats human flesh? Jäger Jane? Yeah right. Well, they all happened. To students all over the country. Not to the masses. But one is too many, isn't it? A

favorite quote of mine is: 'You can't expect to be treated great if you don't first believe that you are great.'

"Alcohol's influence is significant in a majority of all criminal cases. It's the same in the stories you just read. Each offender and each victim definitely drank in excess before taking their first step on the road leading to their unfortunate fates.

"For the record, I like drinking. I may be small, but I can drink like a fish—no pun intended. So travel. Study abroad. Dance on the moon. Trust the majority, just not everybody. Party. Get crazy. Have fun. Live it up and build a billion memories. But love yourselves, and others, please."

Everybody Loves Raymond

When doctors become doctors, they take the Hippocratic oath. Basically, they swear to be ethical, to do no harm, and to treat sick people to the best of their ability.

Believe it or not, teachers also take an oath. Each individual teacher is asked to write their own. Although they may use different words, the message is basically the same: to be ethical, not to harm, and to educate kids as best as they can.

Raymond Westin had been the head of the art department at the local high school since it opened, and he had won the

Golden Apple award more times than any other teacher in the state. His office was always buzzing with students from the opening bell to the end of the school day.

Ritchie was a freshman whose family had just moved to town. He was a great photographer and hoped to take pictures at the football games and join the yearbook club. Mr. Westin let Ritchie use his darkroom to develop his photos.

During first semester, the two became really close. Mr. Westin loved Ritchie's photographs, and he started hanging them up all over the hallways. Ritchie became kind of a celebrity on campus. "Shoot me, shoot me!" kids would say.

One Sunday before Christmas, Mr. Westin invited Ritchie to bring his camera to his apartment to take some pictures of the holiday lights from his balcony. When Ritchie got there, Mr. Westin opened the door in his robe. He was not wearing anything underneath it.

A teacher from Oregon wrote her credo even before she became certified. In it she says, "I always loved kids, but now I will have the chance to contribute to the success and happiness of their future . . ."

Sometimes Golden Apples turn out to be rotten. Speaking of apples, let's check in with an expert. What do you think, Witchiepoo?

"This is what I think, my little pretties. 99.9 percent of the grown-ups in your life will be loving and honorable people. But if there is ever a teacher, coach, family member, neighbor, or anyone who ever makes you feel uncomfortable, makes any type of inappropriate sexual advancements toward you, even if you think it's no big deal, it only happened once, maybe I'm

overreacting, be sure in your mind—here's two numbers to
call. Gotta go now, I'm off to see the wizard."

National Sexual Assault Telephone Hotline: 800-656-4673

Or email Dumbo at rshindler@sbcglobal.net

DRUGS

@420.nation

One of today's great debates around 420 Nation is the question of why marijuana is legal in some states and not legal in others. Can you believe there are more recreational pot shops in Colorado than there are McDonald's and Starbucks locations in the Mile-High State combined? Although cannabis will be legal for recreational use in South Dakota as of July 1, 2021, there was a time not so long ago when you could be sentenced to a year in jail for just living in a place where marijuana is smoked. Which means you and your roommate could have shared a jail cell if he got busted for having weed in your apartment, even if you never took a puff.

On January 20, 2020, Illinois became the eleventh state in America to legalize weed. Later in the year, four additional states followed suit: Arizona, New Jersey, Montana, and South Dakota. They join Alaska, California, Colorado, Maine, Massachusetts, Michigan, Nevada, Oregon, Vermont, Washington, and Washington, DC.

Even though there are small differences in the rules between each state, like how many ounces of cannabis you can have on your person or in your house, every state agrees you have to be twenty-one years old and cannot smoke in any public place—like parks, playgrounds, streets, sidewalks, any businesses, within 1,000 feet of a school or daycare center, amusement parks, carnivals, casinos, bars, lobbies of hotels, in bus stations, on train platforms, movie theaters, schools, near someone who's under twenty-one years of age, close to a bus driver, around a police officer, next to a firefighter, or during Sunday services in church.

So you might be wondering, where the heck can ya take a puff?

"I'll tell you where you absolutely, positively, cannot light up. In your car, that's where. Because if you're going to get caught, this is definitely where it's going to happen 99.9 percent of the time. Some states require you to keep your stash in your locked glove compartment, while others say leave it in your trunk. They all agree on one thing: You can't smoke in your car. Zero Tolerance."

You might be thinking, fine, I'm eighteen and I don't always listen to my parents, but I hear you. I won't light up in my car. What about taking a hit or two before I start driving? I have this friend who knows more about pot than anyone on the planet.

The Guru of Ganga, Master of Marijuana. And she guarantees me it's impossible to get arrested for driving under the influence of cannabis because it's impossible to prove someone is driving high.

"Remember a few pages back when I brought up the buzzer? On a game show like *Jeopardy!* when a contestant gives the wrong answer, there's a buzzer sound that goes off to signify it's a wrong answer. Sounds sort of like *EHnt*. Every time you think of doing something you know in your heart is not right—like posting something private on the Internet, having sex with someone you think may be underage, leaving a bar alone, not checking out who you're swiping right for, taking that one extra shot, not speaking up for another person who's vulnerable, or getting in your car with drugs or alcohol—listen for that *EHnt* sound in your head. It's a radar distinguishing wrong from right, and it's always in there. Sometimes it can help you make a different choice."

It's true, testing for marijuana is difficult, but lots of people are still arrested for driving under the influence of it. Many states make it illegal to have any amount of THC in your blood while you're driving. So even that quick hit from your one-hitter can still be enough to charge you. The state of the stoner movement is really dazed and confused, and its laws are just too new and too complicated to take a chance.

Joey the Joint

I won't smoke before I get in my car. Or while I'm driving. I'll just keep the joint in my pocket until I get home.

Not so fast . . .

Mariah was a junior in college studying architecture. Like one of the skyscrapers she dreamed of building one day, her future seemed sky-high. After finals, she and her three suitemates jumped in her Mercury Mountaineer and took off on an excursion to The Lost Railway Museum in Michigan. Mariah had been obsessed with trains and locomotives since she was a kid.

They walked around the entire museum from top to bottom two separate times. After leaving, they picked up a half pint of Fireball whiskey, and Mariah parked their car inside the most beautiful park you could ever imagine.

While staring at the clouds, Mariah took a sip and passed the bottle over to Ava, who took a shot and handed it back. Before Mariah could lift the bottle to take another drink, a park officer rode up on his twenty-one-speed bike. While patting her down for having open alcohol in the car, Bicycle Bob discovered a joint inside Mariah's front pocket. Both she and her friends were brought to a police station right outside Lansing. Fortunately for her fellow architects-to-be, they were let go without being charged. Mariah was not so lucky—she was charged with possession of marijuana.

You might be thinking, *wait, isn't marijuana legal in Michigan?*

"Yes, sort of."

And Mariah wasn't smoking the joint, was she? Then why does she still get arrested for it?

"Because even though the sixteen states, including Michigan, have legalized pot, the federal government still has not. Some land is owned by the state government, and some land is owned by the federal government.

"So although, Michigan's law says it's legal to possess recreational marijuana all over its 96,716-square-mile state, if you're standing on a piece of land in Michigan owned by the federal government, you're busted!"

If you don't understand the distinction, join the club! Nobody does. Something should either be legal or illegal, yes? Creating this grayness catches pot smokers right in the center of the purple haze.

"Maybe someday after Mariah becomes an architect, she can build a time machine so we can travel back and figure out what lawmakers were thinking. I know it's confusing. And it's easy to say 'Don't ever carry or smoke marijuana outside;' it's also unrealistic. Some of you are going to smoke, and sometimes you'll do it outside. Some examples of land owned by the federal government are things like parks, forest preserves, lakes, some beaches, and other outdoor places where a lot of marijuana is smoked. So just know the risks, know who you're with, where you are, and listen for the EHnt."

Rob Shindler

Dude, Where's My Car?

Some Gen Zers ask me, "What if I'm not the one holding the drugs? What if it's my passenger? And what if I don't even know he or she's got it? Or what if I don't even know what drug it even is?"

"According to the Stanford Open Policing Project, police pull over more than 50,000 drivers on a typical day and more than 20,000,000 motorists every year. One of the most common reasons people get arrested by the police starts or has something do with a traffic stop—and over a third of these traffic stops lead to DUI investigations and discovering drugs in a car.

"So whether it's marijuana, cocaine, or heroin, if you're going to get caught, it's almost always going to happen in a car. And it's usually going to happen after you give the police probable cause to pull your car over. Unless an officer has a warrant signed by a judge, under the Fourth Amendment of the US Constitution, they cannot stop your car, search it or you, without first having probable cause.

"In other words, they need a reason to stop people. Speeding, going through a stoplight, blowing off a stop sign, changing lanes without using a turn signal, or simply having something hanging from your rearview mirror like air fresheners, parking permits, the garage door opener, the rosary beads your grandma gave you as a present. Wait, there's more . . . Tinted windows, a crack in your windshield, snow or ice you don't properly remove from your window in the wintertime, the plastic figurine of a hula dancer you won at the carnival last summer. Any violation.

"Once they have that, anything illegal they find can change the course of your night and possibly your life. Besides the possibility of getting arrested and taken to jail, someone is also likely going to need to start riding the train, taking a bus, or calling an Uber, because someone could be looking at losing their car."

Eddie loved his car. He had just bought it a month before. It was a used Cadillac Escalade, but it looked brand new. Black on black. Loaded. The kind of truck everyone noticed when it came cruising down the street. He had been saving up since he got his permit. Eddie washed it more than most teenagers shower.

One day, Eddie's best friend Danny needed a ride to work.

"Can we make a quick stop on the way?" he asked. "Not long, maybe ten minutes." Parked across from the apartment building, Eddie waited outside listening to his new stereo. It was so loud he didn't even flinch when the two undercover cars pulled up behind him.

Turns out, Danny's quick ten-minute stop was to meet with an undercover officer posing as a buyer for a pound of weed. After the deal went down, Danny was handcuffed and escorted outside to meet up with the others. Eddie's Escalade was already being loaded onto the tow truck.

Did he know Danny was making a drug deal? Maybe, maybe not. It doesn't matter. If the police think he did, that's all the probable cause or proof they need for an arrest. And even though they don't find the drugs in the car, they can still take it, because in the eyes of the law, the Escalade was used to transport or bring the drugs to the undercover officer. It will be eight months and $8,500 later until Eddie hears the sounds of that stereo again.

Poor Papa

Lara worked part time at a travel agency after school. Every Christmas she flew to a different sunny destination with the help of her 20 percent employee discount. The previous December it was Hawaii. The next year, Jamaica. She had recently lost her mom and her father was heartbroken. They'd been together since grammar school.

She decided to surprise him. Under the tree with a red bow wrapped around it was his plane ticket. She hadn't seen him smile like that in a long, long time.

The pot in Jamaica was so good—too good not to bring back home. TSA never even smelled the stuff Lara carefully stashed inside her make-up bag next to her lipstick and eyeliner.

A few weeks later, Lara was driving back from the mall in her father's car and was pulled over for changing lanes without signaling. After exiting the vehicle, the officer asked to check Lara's purse.

Did he have a right to do this? Maybe, maybe not. But this argument will have to wait to be made until she goes to court.

Inside her purse he found a joint some little leaguers could use as a baseball bat. That was not the problem, though. It was the coke he found in her compact case. Not a lot, but enough. He took her into custody and had the car—her dad's car—towed to the police pound. Her dad hired a lawyer and spent the next few months trying to save his car from being forfeited to the state. It was the only way he got to work and visited the cemetery where Lara's mom is buried.

Lucky Number Six

Stuart had recently been voted social chairman of his fraternity. His duties included planning the parties, getting the food, and picking up beer from the liquor store.

One weekend, he was put in charge of getting some cocaine. Not a lot, just a few grams. Lucas was joining him on the quest. Luke was Stuart's roommate and was majoring in theatre. He was starring in the university's production of *Beauty and the Beast*. Unknown to Stuart, Luke also secretly had a history with the guy they're getting the stuff from.

They drove forty minutes out of town. When they arrived, Jason met them in the underground parking lot. He handed

Stuart a small envelope. Stu passed three hundred-dollar bills, but Jason refused to take them.

"It's cool bud." he said. "On me this time. I told Brad Pitt over there all you gotta do is bring this bag back with you, someone will text you where to meet. Easy peasy, right?" Stuart looked over at Lucas who nervously nodded his head up and down like a toy robot on extra-strength batteries.

Heading back to campus, they were pulled over by an undercover SUV for having expired license plates. A few minutes later, two more arrived. After being yanked from the driver's seat, the agent brought Stuart back to the rear of his Jeep.

"What's in the bag, big man?" he asked.

"I have no idea," Stu stuttered.

The two agents in the first SUV had been tapping his phone and monitoring Jason's movements for over a year. Lucas and Jason actually sat next to each other back in elementary school. Now the two, along with Stuart, will unfortunately sit side-by-side-by-side at a table together in front of a judge in court. Ironically, six was Stuart's lucky number. That's how many kilos were found in the black duffel. You don't need to be a math wizard to know that's a whole lot of heroin. Enough to change the course of someone's life. Stuart's life.

The US government has mandatory minimum penalties for certain drug offenses. The duffel found in Stuart's trunk carries a minimum sentence of ten years in jail.

Stuart finished an internship last summer with General Electric. They loved him and offered him a job after graduation. They offered him a $90,000 starting salary. However, GE doesn't hire drug dealers. After learning about the arrest, they pulled their offer. They also placed Stuart on the do-not-hire list.

"How many different ways can I tell you that you should have nothing illegal inside your vehicle? Never, never, never, never, never, never. That's six, which I'm guessing may no longer be Stu's lucky number. If he heard the buzzer in his head before buying the coke and loading the bag in his trunk, things could have been different. You're going to make choices, good and bad. Just please don't let the bad ones happen inside your car."

Up, Up, and Away

Next week is spring break. Skiing in Colorado. You can't wait to hit the slopes—or visit that new dispensary, Green Dragon. You get a free joint and a grinder with the store's logo on it when you spend over one hundred dollars. Just like Lara, you're planning on bringing home some leftovers in your purse or stashing two or three vape pens inside your computer case. After all, pot is now legal in your state, so you can travel with it on the airplane, right?

"While you're up, up, up and away in the friendly skies, you could be crossing unfriendly airspace into states like Nebraska, Missouri, or Florida, where recreational marijuana has not yet been legalized. Just like Mariah inside the park, airplanes and airspace in the sky are regulated by the federal government. So for the brief time your jet is flying through Nebraska on the way back to Chicago, the marijuana hiding out in your purse is violating the law. When you land, if the police or TSA find it, you can be arrested. I know, the chances of you getting caught seem slim. Maybe one in a million. Sounds like pretty good odds. Unless you're the one. Education is power. Know the risks before taking off."

Pineapple Express

Every year, Toby struggled with what to get his cousin for his birthday. The year before, his gift of a favorite fruit of the month club subscription bombed. The next year, he wanted to nail it.

Toby lived in Seattle where recreational marijuana is legal. His cousin lived in Florida, where it's not. Toby got a great idea for a gift. He put four grams of sativa inside a small container. Then, he placed the small container in a cardboard box. He put the cardboard box inside a slightly bigger cardboard box. Finally, he sealed it all up underneath a bunch of his cousin's favorite red licorice inside a fourth box. That Toby was one sly magician.

He took it to the post office, and off the package went. So did his cell phone when his cousin called telling him he had never spent a birthday at the police station.

"As with airplanes, post offices are run by the federal government, and if you send something illegal in the mail, like pot or another drug, both the sender and receiver can be criminally charged with a federal offense. So send a card, send a cake, send a pineapple. Just please don't send drugs."

In school, you had a class where you learned about the different branches of our government. There's the federal government and the state government. During the COVID-19 crisis, we heard a lot about this distinction and the arguments of who should and would make certain decisions. Our legal system has two sets of laws—federal law and state law. Federal laws apply to the entire country, all fifty states. State laws apply to each individual state. Every state has their own rules. When there's a conflict between a state law and a federal law, like legalizing marijuana, federal law wins. Being arrested is being arrested. It stinks! What you're doing and where you're doing it determines who's putting the handcuffs on.

Jumpin' Jack Flash

According to the National Highway Traffic Safety Administration, about 1.5 million people will be arrested this year for driving under the influence of alcohol. There's no excuse, no explanation, no justification, for anyone to ever get a DUI.

Here's why:

- Uber
- Lyft
- Curb
- Mytaxi
- Flywheel
- Juno

- Easytaxi
- Arro
- Safr
- Via
- Fasten
- Gett

- A cousin, a friend, an uncle, a coworker, a neighbor . . . a crazy ex-girlfriend

Just like with pot, coke, and any other drug, there is never a reason to get behind the wheel of a car after drinking alcohol.

If Uber, Lyft, or the crazy ex cannot keep you out of the car, maybe two other emotions can: greed and fear.

By the time you're done with a lawyer, a judge, and Tony the tow truck driver, your DUI arrest will cost you almost $10,000, if not more.

Maybe you have a trust fund or still keep your tooth fairy savings under your pillow. So, perhaps money is not a concern. How do you feel about privacy? There are no doors on the bathroom stalls in jail.

Stephen was a sophomore playing soccer at the University of Indiana. His season had just ended, and he and his two friends decided to take a road trip to Wisconsin to visit a few high school buddies. They stopped at Big Red Liquors and picked up a twelve pack. They should have made it to Madison before noon.

Steve didn't even see the other car change lanes. By the time the police arrived on the scene, Kyle was already gone.

He was the passenger in front and was launched out from the sunroof. He would've turned nineteen years old next week. In back was Alberto. Thankfully, he survived. He would never walk again, though.

In a flash, Stephen lost his dear friend and was about to lose his freedom. Besides a felony aggravated operating while intoxicated causing injuries charge, Steve was also charged with first degree reckless homicide. Under Section 940.02 of the Wisconsin Statutes, reckless homicide is punishable by up to sixty years in prison. Steve could be close to eighty years old before getting out.

Speaking of close to eighty years old, look who just walked in. It's Grandpa Dumbo. Gramps, how could Steve be arrested when the accident wasn't even his fault? The other driver veered into his lane forcing him off the road.

"Doesn't matter. His blood alcohol concentration was .11, greater than the legal limit in every state in the country. Liability or responsibility in an accident is irrelevant if the party not at fault is determined to be drunk. My all-time favorite rock star, Mick Jagger, who just happens to be a few months older than me, has a favorite saying: 'Lose your dreams, and you might lose your mind.' Well, drive drunk or high, and you could lose both. Listen for the EHnt."

Behind the Eight Ball

Let me be honest. That is certainly not your average, everyday DUI. This one was a whopper. Most DUI cases are just everyday cheeseburgers that thankfully don't result in injuries, death, or jail. They're much simpler. Like Derek's.

Although you won't see him on ESPN, Derek could hold his own against most amateur pool players. He sometimes walked out with over $200 in winnings. Not bad for a college sophomore. One night in October was no exception. He was killing it, even after eight beers. In between games, he ran out to his car to use the charger to juice up his phone. He didn't turn the motor on, just twisted the key so the battery would work. He walked back inside to start his next game.

About forty-five minutes later, he went outside to grab his phone. Parked behind him was a squad car. Derek had no idea why the cop was there, but it was freezing so he hurried into the driver's seat and closed the door.

The officer knocked on the window with her flashlight. She noticed the bloodshot eyes and odor of alcohol, so she asked Derek to step out of the car. After doing some sobriety tests in the parking lot, she put Derek in handcuffs and placed him under arrest for driving under the influence of alcohol. At the station, Derek took the breathalyzer and blew a .15 result—almost double the legal limit.

Some of you might be thinking, *what the heck! Derek wasn't even driving. The car wasn't moving. The engine wasn't even turned on. Can you explain this to us?*

"It doesn't matter. Sitting drunk behind the steering wheel with the keys in the ignition is enough to allow the police to arrest you. Believe it or not, there are cases where someone who has been drinking pulls off the road and falls asleep in the backseat of the car with the keys in their pocket, not in the ignition. They can still be arrested for DUI."

But they're passed out, not even in the front seat.

"Under the law, they still have control over the vehicle. In other words, at any time they could wake up, take the keys out of their pocket, start the engine, and drive away. It may not make any sense, but neither does getting in your car and driving after you have been drinking. That's why I keep using the phrase Zero Tolerance."

What if I'm really, really careful, and I'm only a few blocks from home?

"Life's full of tough choices. Right, Ursula?"

Say a Little Prayer for Me

Ursula was an amazing driver. She didn't get even one ticket since passing her driving test. That was why her parents surprised her with a car when she turned twenty-one.

She had four tequila and sodas at the party, but she parked less than a mile from her dorm. She could literally see the roof of her building. Remember, Ursula was an amazing driver.

"Ursula was the best student in our driver's ed class. Graduated with honors. Everything's perfect. Just like we taught her. Seatbelt on, lights activated, side mirrors adjusted. She'll be in her cozy bed under her warm blanket in a matter of moments. If she's not too tired, maybe she can even have a slice of the homemade blueberry pie her mom sent before falling asleep."

Ursula was operating her vehicle flawlessly. Speed limit was forty miles per hour. She was going thirty-nine miles per hour. She was staying in the center of her lane, both hands were on the steering wheel in the nine and three position. Ursula really was an amazing driver. And a good Catholic.

When she got the car, her grandma gave her a beautiful strand of rosary beads to wrap around the rearview mirror.

They'll keep her safe and always be a constant reminder of her sweet nanna.

Ursula may have been an amazing driver, but Officer Friendly had amazing eyes. A block from the dorm, the patrol car noticed those red and black rosary beads hanging from the mirror.

Under the law, a police officer can make a traffic stop if he or she has a reasonable suspicion that something hanging from around or under the rearview mirror obstructs the driver's view.

Ursula was pulled over, and after doing slightly worse than Derek did on his sobriety tests, she was arrested for driving under the influence. The officer allowed her to take the strand of rosary beads with her before placing her in the squad car. After all, she'll need all the help she can get.

Wine into Water

Word on the street is you can never be guilty of DUI if you pass the breathalyzer test. Izzy, what do you think?

Izzy was twenty-four years old, but she had just started college a few months before at the state university about three hours from her home. She delayed this next chapter of her life because her mom had been ill, and Izzy chose to stay back to take care of her. Thankfully, her mom made a full recovery. Now, it was time for Izzy to launch her dream of becoming a nurse. Izzy was the oldest freshman on campus.

While taking care of her mom, Izzy spent lots of nights getting to know some new friends. Cabernet. Merlot. Pinot noir. Shiraz. Zinfandel. She had it down to a science. Drink three or four glasses of wine followed by a chaser of one liter of water. Never failed.

Blending the water with the wine somehow canceled each of the glasses out, miraculously making Izzy's blood alcohol level register under the legal limit of .08. At least that was what Izzy's cousin Patty the paralegal swore to. She guaranteed you can never get arrested for DUI if your blood alcohol level is under the legal limit.

EHnt.

After pulling her over for weaving between lanes, an officer noticed Izzy's bloodshot eyes and slurred speech. She also had a tough time finding her license in her wallet and used the door for balance when getting out of the car. Even though she only blew a .06, under the legal limit, she was still arrested and charged with DUI.

Please, just make it a rule—regardless of how much you drink or what someone else tells you, never get in your car. Or someone else's after they've been drinking.

Shotgun Shelley

Once upon a time, there was a little girl named Shelley. Even though Shelley was the youngest of four, she never lost the shotgun family battle. Not a single time. Regardless of where they were going, the second she and her sisters stepped out of the apartment complex heading toward their mom's car, she screamed "Shotgun!" Which meant she got to sit in the front seat. She earned her nickname—Shotgun Shelley.

The title stuck and followed her all the way into high school. She may not have had a car like some of her friends, but she was always the co-pilot. Shotgun and her crew went everywhere together, including Gwen's party one Saturday.

Someone always volunteered to be the designated driver. That night, the job went to Trisha. She picked everyone up in her Mazda Miata. Four squeezed into the back, Shelley of course, slid in the front. Even though it was getting dark outside, they were all wearing sunglasses and bikinis—it was a beach theme. Everybody from their class was invited, and Gwen's backyard was transformed into a Caribbean resort filled with sand, tiki lights, volleyball nets, and Jell-O shots. People were getting trashed, including the designated driver.

The party was still going strong at 1:30 a.m. when the girls decided to leave. Actually, Shelley was the only one who was sober; she only had one beer because she was planning to study all Sunday for the ACT. It was her fourth time sitting for the test. Normally, she would take over for Trish, but the Mazda was a manual and Shelley didn't know how to drive stick.

It was like the tree came out of nowhere.

"There's not a lot of nevers in this world. You never tell a shark they look fat in that outfit. You never let a friend leave a bar alone. You never turn down free pizza. You never get behind the wheel if you've been drinking or have drugs on you. And you never get in a car knowing that the driver is intoxicated."

The last time Shelley's mom received such a call was when she found out her daughters' dad was killed by a drunk driver. That was almost fifteen years ago. Trish had lost control coming out of the cul-de-sac. Thirty seconds after leaving the party. That oak tree had been part of the neighborhood for over five decades. All the damage was to the front passenger side of the car.

It took the fire department nearly an hour to get Shelley out. She would be okay, but she'd need three or four operations and lots of therapy. The Mazda Miata wasn't so lucky. It looked like an elephant stepped on it.

Thankfully, nobody else had been injured. Of course, Trish was arrested and the next year or so of her life would be spent going back and forth to court. Obviously, she'll also forever be remorseful for hurting her friend. They met in the sandbox in preschool.

That's not the point of this particular tale.

"Friends don't let friends drive drunk. But they also don't get into a car with someone who they know has been drinking. Zero Tolerance. Translation: Never! Listen, I get

it. FOMO—Fear of Missing Out. I remember lots of times I'd paddle up to the shallow end with some of the squid and snails to check out a new clam bar. I didn't want to miss a second of fun. But every so often, you have to hear that voice in your head (EHnt) telling you this may be the one time you don't have to join in. Sometimes the possible risks outweigh the possible rewards. You always have options. Choices. Even if you have to make that dreadful call at 1:30 a.m. in the morning, a parent would much rather pick you up from a party than meet you at the hospital."

Addie Adderall

Neena was a genius. The real deal. An Einstein. She officially tested as a genius back in third grade. As a junior at U of G, she was now surrounded by other geniuses who also finished at the top of their high school classes. Together, they started their own club called Ladies Llaredda. Coincidentally, llaredda is *Adderall* spelled backwards.

Here's how it worked: Pop a pill after dinner, party until midnight, then back to the library where they study until dawn. Perfect recipe for success. Who says you can't have it all?

You've heard all the noise about taking drugs. The risks, the dangers. But this drug is legit—just like the Mensa test they all shattered back in grade school. Studies show how it improves attention and focus and reduces impulsive behaviors. It's all true. Hear it from the horse's mouth.

"Hello ladies. I, too, finished at the top of my class. So that makes two things we have in common. Brains and beauty. Remember when we first met I said sometimes I can actually be kind of funny? The class clown. Well, I think it's time for a little joke. Ready?"

Sure.

"Knock knock."

Who's there?

"Girl on Adderall who went to a job interview."

Girl on Adderall who went to a job interview who?

"Girl on Adderall who went to a job interview and after taking a drug test got tossed out of the vice president's office and lost the $125,000 starting salary, that's who."

Wait a second. Why?

"It's true, Adderall has amazing results with kids who have ADHD. But Adderall and methamphetamine also belong to the same class of drugs and have similar chemical structures. Adderall comes up as crystal meth on a drug test. So when the company got back the results, they just assumed Neena was a meth head. They validated her parking ticket and sent her on her way."

You know any other jokes?

"What did the horse say when it fell?"

I don't know, what did the horse say when it fell?

"I've fallen and I can't giddyup!"

Lose by a Hair

"Friends, Romans, countrymen. Lend me your ears. Allow me to please educate you on the highs and lows of marijuana in the workplace. Theo was up for this big job. His letters of recommendations were stellar. His grades were impeccable. He was the number one candidate for the position. All he needed to do was ace the interview and pass the drug test."

So tell us, what happened?

"Theo smoked a lot of pot. I mean, a lot. One of his roommates who was in pre-med gave him some tips on how to make sure he beat the drug test."

Go on.

"You see, there's no exact way to know how long weed stays in your system. Lots of different things go into it. Like how often you smoke, how much you weigh, how strong the stuff is that you're smoking."

And?

"Well, if you only smoke on the weekends, it could be out of your system in a few days. But if you light up every night, it could stay in there for a month."

So all Theo has to do to pass the test is stay clean for thirty days, right?

"That's if you take the urine test. It is a different story if they perform a blood test."

Well?

"Statistics show it could be sixty to seventy-five days for a blood test. Just to be safe, his roommate tells him no smoking for two and a half months, then the job is his. So that's what he did. Not a huff or a puff for seventy-six days."

Woo hoo, Theo! How did he celebrate after he got the job?

"He didn't get it. Doctor-To-Be Roomie forgot to tell him about the dreaded hair follicle test. They remove a small amount of hair from your head, and it can show smoking for the past ninety days, sometimes even longer. When you have a question about Shakespeare, ask your English teacher. When it's something legal, talk with a lawyer."

Grannie's Zannies

Even as a lawyer, I had no idea how popular Xanax is in today's culture. I remember my mom taking one pill at night to help her sleep. These days, kids are sneaking into grandma's medicine cabinet stealing some from her prescription bottles. There are so many benefits of the drug for people who struggle with anxiety, panic attacks, and insomnia. But there's also legal risks you should know and understand, like being arrested for driving under the influence of a prescription drug.

"Hold on a second. I'm a medicine prescribed by a doctor. What's so illegal about that?"

Well first, if you steal it from Nanna's bathroom or buy it off the street, it's not really a legal prescription. And second, there's Zero Tolerance. In other words, if it's in your system while you're driving and you get caught, it's a DUI. Different drug, same rule. Nothing illegal in you or in your car.

When misused, like mixing it with alcohol, Xanax can cause a train wreck.

Joey and Mason had been friends since second grade. They vowed to someday stand in each other's weddings. Joey never thought his best bro would have been capable of doing something like this.

Twenty minutes after secretly slipping the little yellow pill into the solo cup, Mason and the others watched Joey have a complete personality transformation. Normally mild mannered, Joey leaped from the lawn chair, tore his T-shirt to shreds like the Hulk, and jumped off the second-floor balcony of the frat house.

That was the last anyone saw of him until the following morning in court at his bond hearing. He was charged with three separate felonies, including home invasion. Somehow, he ended up inside an apartment building banging on the door of 17B. When the tenant refused to let him in, Joey kicked open the door, leaving a two-inch gash under the guy's eye. Joey had no memory of any of this.

Home invasion is a class X felony punishable by six to thirty years in jail.

"Before you drop a yellow pill in someone's drink . . . before you turn into the Hulk . . . before you break into someone else's house . . . please hear the EHnt!"

For questions or concerns on teen drug abuse, contact the National Drug Hotline at 844-289-0879.

Or email Dumbo at rshindler@sbcglobal.net.

ETC, ETC, ETC.

105.2

Ivan was driving home from visiting his sister in Indiana. His GPS must have had too many beers itself, because it took him way out of the way from his home in Chicago. He was already forty minutes past curfew. He didn't even know his mom's Honda could go one hundred miles per hour.

"You were going over 105 miles per hour! You think you're racing in the final lap of the Indianapolis 500, son?" the officer asked after pulling him over.

"If I'm home after 12:30 a.m., my parents are going to kill me," Ivan answered as he gave him his license and proof of insurance.

The officer laughed as he walked back to his squad car. *Maybe he'll cut me a break*, Ivan thought to himself. No such luck. A few minutes later, the officer returned and handed him the $750 ticket. His father really was going to kill him.

From the very first time you sit in the car behind the steering wheel on your mom or dad's lap making the *vroom, vroom* sound, the dream of driving is born. Unlike most exams, the test at the DMV is the one teenagers can't wait to take.

Ivan decided to hide the ticket in his sock drawer. All his friends kept telling him to just pay the $750 fine and do the eight hours of traffic school online. Nobody had to know. Great advice, right?

Let's check in with a professional.

"Don't ever just pay the fine. Always go to court. Here's why. What if the officer doesn't show up? Maybe the ticket gets thrown out. Even if they are there, in person you always have the chance to look a judge in the eye and ask them for mercy."

Some of you might be wondering if you should go to court alone or bring a lawyer. What do you think, Dumbo?

"It depends on the type of ticket you got. If it's something simple like going through a stop sign or stoplight, especially if there wasn't an accident, many times you can actually resolve this by yourself. For more serious offenses, you should hire a lawyer. A lawyer can talk with the prosecutor (the attorney for the state) and try to work out a better deal for you to protect your license. The better deal might be reducing the charge, getting supervision, and avoiding a conviction.

Things that you may not be able to do yourself. Every case is different. Here's some advice: talk with family members or friends—believe me, everyone knows a lawyer. There are lots out there. Some would even say too many! Having this referral or introduction allows you to feel comfortable and know you will be treated fairly. Also, when a potential client is sent by someone a lawyer knows or even loves, a lawyer feels a sense of responsibility to take care of, protect, and not overcharge the person. You can ask a few questions, get a quote, and hopefully hear their opinion if you do or do not need their services. It's worth making a phone call or two just to have the conversation—knowledge is power!"

Should I Stay or Should I Go?

"Should I Stay or Should I Go" is a song written in 1981 by the punk rock band The Clash. *Rolling Stone* ranks it as one of the top 250 songs of all time.

When it comes to a car accident, the answer is always, always, always stay.

Recently, an eighteen year old was driving home from school and went through a stop sign; she accidentally hit a little boy crossing the street. She was so nervous, she drove away and left the kid laying there unconscious. An ambulance eventually came; the little boy was in a coma at the hospital.

"You might be wondering, *Is she a criminal?* We could agree to disagree on that question. Personally, I see her as a scared teenager who had two choices.

1. Stop, call 911, and wait.

2. Or run.

Choosing choice number one gets her a ticket and a $50 fine. Number two changes the course of her life. She's charged with a felony punishable by three to seven years in jail.

If the little boy dies, God forbid, she could be charged with leaving the scene of an accident involving a death or even reckless homicide.

Even if you hit an unoccupied car only causing minor damage to the door and nobody's around to even see it, you should leave a note with your name and number. There's no gray area to being honorable. *EHnt . . .*"

Maggie the Murderer

Merriam-Webster defines *conspiracy* as "an illegal, treasonable, or treacherous plan to harm or destroy another person, group, or entity."

"For example, you, me, and our friend, Margaret, decided to rob the 7/11

on the corner. You drove the getaway car, Maggie was the lookout, and I had the gun. I ordered the cashier to open the register. When he refused, I accidentally pulled the trigger. The clerk died before the paramedics arrived."

You and Maggie could never be charged with murder, right? Wrong.

"All for one and one for all. We don't get to the store without your car. Margaret was standing outside the front door watching for the police, and I'm the Dummy who took a husband from his wife and a father from his kids. At the station, we were all fingerprinted and charged with felony murder.

"Felony murder applies when someone kills another person while committing a crime that goes bad, even if they never planned on killing anyone. The offender and their accomplices (yep, you and Maggie) can all be found guilty of murder. If it seems like it's a bad plan and it sounds like it's a bad plan, it probably is!"

Quintin was thirteen years old. After his dad died from a sudden heart attack, Q was lost. Until he was found. A recruiter from the neighborhood gang invited him to join.

Quintin was the third-youngest member of the gang, but he caught on fast. At the beginning, he was just doing marijuana drops from one block to another. Like a baton runner in a relay race, Q was flawless in handing off the weed for the cash.

In the spring, he was promoted to guns. Q had been arrested for a few minor things. Disorderly conduct, trespassing, drinking alcohol in public. The charges were always dropped. He never served a day in jail.

His first real bust was at a gas station when an undercover officer noticed the bulge of a gun in Quintin's pocket. Strike two came on New Year's Eve when Q celebrated by shooting his gun up in the air. That time, he was arrested and charged. He pled guilty and got probation. He was required to wear an ankle bracelet and had a curfew.

He was doing really well with his probation. Only sixty-one days left. Then, like when you eat ice cream too fast, Q got a brain freeze. He cut the bracelet from his left ankle with his mom's garden shears and went off the radar.

Q snuck up on a shed and shot a rival gang member in the head. Three times. It took the police two hours to find him hiding out in his basement. He still had the gun in his school backpack.

"Too little knowledge is dangerous. Everyone kept assuring Q that juveniles are off-limits. That they're never arrested; that they never go to jail. Quintin was charged with attempted murder . . . as an adult. The case is resolved downtown in the main criminal courthouse, not the juvenile detention center in the suburbs. Quintin gets nineteen years in prison. He'll be out when he's thirty-five years old. The same age his dad was when he died."

Dirty Doug

Over the last thirty years, I have represented thousands and thousands of people in the Hispanic community. During these years, I've seen a novel's worth of injustice. Here's only one of many.

Fernando was thirty-two years old and worked as a foreman in a factory. Together, he and his wife, Angelina, had four children between the ages of three and thirteen years old. Fernando was a wonderful husband and dad who worked seven days a week supporting his family. He had an infectious laugh that filled every crack in the three bedrooms of their home.

One night after work, he and his brother-in-law stopped at a local bar to pick up a six pack to go. Twenty seconds later, a drunk, off-duty police officer pointed his gun at Fernando's head.

Officer Doug had had two shots of bourbon and seven beers, and he thought the two men were robbing the place. It was all captured on surveillance video.

Charges were filed against the officer, and a hearing was set to suspend him for one year. Fernando was subpoenaed to be a witness. Before the hearing, an investigation was performed—on Fernando, of all people! They discover he had two prior convictions from when he was a teenager for nonviolent offenses. He hadn't had any legal problems for over ten years.

After Officer Doug was cleared of all charges, Fernando left the courthouse. Outside waiting for him in front were Immigration and Customs Enforcement (ICE) agents. Eventually, Fernando was deported back to Mexico. Many believe the officer from the bar was the one who actually called ICE. Fernando's wife had to sell their house.

"If you're an immigrant in the United States without your legal immigration papers, you are definitely held to a higher standard. You cannot get arrested. For anything. The truth is, it's not just the Fernandos of our world who need to stay clean. We all do. I know as teenagers and young adults, it's pretty hard to picture yourself being thirty-two years old. It seems like a billion years away. But what you do today can crumble your tomorrow."

Before falling asleep every night, Fernando always kissed his youngest daughter Lizzie on both cheeks and whispered, "Te amo de aquí a la luna." (I love you from here to the moon.)

After all this, he may never get to do that again.

La-La

In the song, "All I Want For Christmas," Alvin and the Chipmunks sing about a little girl whose only wish is getting her two front teeth. When she turned seventeen, this girl's list changed.

"All I want for Christmas is my fake ID."

Just like sixteen year olds can't wait to get behind the steering wheel, twenty-one year olds can't wait to get into a bar. Most teenagers can't wait that long. So before Venmoing your hard-earned $85.00 to Chengdu, China, for your counterfeit identification card, at least know the risks.

In most states, anyone convicted of possessing or using a fraudulent driver's license or ID card will receive a one-year suspension of their driving privileges. In addition, you could also face up to one to three years in jail and pay a minimum fine of $500. Truth is, 99 percent of the time, these serious penalties will never happen, especially for first-time offenders. But there are more ramifications than just losing your license.

When you send away for a fake ID, you give your personal information to these people, which puts you at risk for identity theft. You could tank your credit score before even getting your first job.

Kayla knew this and was too smart to risk sending away for a fake. She had a much better plan.

Kayla was a senior in high school and had just gotten accepted into the University of North Carolina where she was planning to join her older sister Chloe the next year. Even though there was a two-year age difference between them, the two were almost identical. People were constantly confusing them for twins.

La-la, Kayla's nickname since first grade, convinced her sister to loan her her driver's license when she was home for winter break. Kayla held it up to the mirror and smiled as she put on the finishing make-up touches before meeting her friends at the bar. She couldn't believe how much they looked like each other. They even had the same widow's peak in the center of their hairlines.

The bouncer looked like a WWE wrestler. He also happened to be an off-duty police officer who received training in how to spot a fake ID.

La-la thought to herself, *Wait a second. This ain't fake. It is real. In fact, my sister just renewed it last August before the se-mester started. And we look just like each other. Identical. She's even wearing my pink sweater in the photo. The one she snuck in her suitcase before leaving for Chapel Hill. I'm safe, right?*

"Nope. Besides being an off-duty police officer and professional wrestler impersonator, Big John was also the father of three daughters. The youngest just happened to be eighteen years old. The same age as Kayla. He had a hunch and acted on it."

"What year were you born, Chloe?" he asked. She stammered, only for a millisecond, enough for his suspicions to be answered.

Kayla cracked and came clean. The officer tossed the license in a box behind the counter filled with a bunch of other plastic cards. Thankfully, he was not going to arrest her and file mis-demeanor charges, but he planned to contact the Secretary of

State Police who will enter one year suspensions against *both* licenses. No good deed goes unpunished. Chloe let her sister use the license knowing she was underage and heading to a bar. She's equally culpable under the law. She was definitely not giving back that sweater now.

"Almost every pre-twenty-one year old is going to at least think about getting a fake ID. Knowing the possible risks is important. Being able to tell the difference between a pro wrestler and a police officer can save you from being knocked out."

BYOB

Aside from having an older sister, Lala also had a younger brother. Unlike Kayla, though, seventeen-year-old Kendall Henderson looked much older. He was 6'4" and started shaving in junior high. He had been dating the same girl he walked to grammar school with.

Kendall picked Dana up for their date at 7:00 p.m. Before leaving his house, he filled his Swell water bottle with pinot grigio, her favorite wine. It took them less than ten minutes to get to the BYOB restaurant. According to Dana's friend, this place never checked IDs.

A few minutes after asking the bus boy for two empty glasses, the manager comes over to their table.

"Good evening, sir. Can I see some ID?"

"Why?" Kendall asked.

"What's in the thermos?" he asked.

"Um. It's, uhh, it's water," Kendall responded.

"You brought your own water to a restaurant?" the manager challenged.

Eventually, Kendall caved. Luckily, the manager only asked them to leave the restaurant. He could have called the police, and Kendall and Dana would have been arrested and charged with possession of alcohol by a minor. Praise the Lord, looks like there would not be another license lost in the Henderson household.

Or would there?

On the way home, they parked on a side street for an hour or so and each one had a few sips of the wine. Eventually, Kendall started the engine and heads off to Dana's. Two blocks later, the squad car pulled them over. Kendall's mom's right taillight was burned out.

Kendall was transferred to the station and booked for driving under the influence of alcohol. That might sound like outer space law. He only had a few sips of the wine and was driving perfectly.

"First, remember any violation gives the police probable cause to pull you over—including a broken taillight. Second, for drivers under the age of twenty-one years old, the law is Zero Tolerance, which means any amount of alcohol found in your system while driving is enough evidence for you to be charged with a DUI.

"There is a small silver lining. The sixty-year-old beer belly patrolman chose not to give Kendall a ticket for having open alcohol in his car. As he put him in the back of his squad car, he sarcastically said, 'Pinot whatever the heck you were drinking isn't really liquor anyways . . .'"

You might be wondering what would've happened if Kendall hadn't taken one sip of the wine and Dana was the only one drinking in the car. Who could be charged with open alcohol?

"Kendall. Under the law, the driver controls what happens in the car. So even if a passenger is the only person drinking, the driver is still the one charged with having open alcohol."

Sphenopalatine Ganglioneuralgia

Sphenopalatine ganglioneuralgia is the scientific name for a brain freeze. You know, when you eat ice cream really fast and it feels like your brain is going to explode. Martin must have swallowed a whole gallon of chocolate chip mint to think this plan would work.

Marty was a waiter at a sushi restaurant. His best friend's uncle actually owned the place. He had been killing it the past few weeks. Marty was a good waiter, but he was not that good. Every Saturday from 5:00 p.m. to 7:00 p.m. was half price on all rolls, so a lot of older couples came in.

Behind the counter was the lost and found where things customers forgot were held. Glasses, phones, keys. And credit cards.

When someone forgot to take their credit card back after paying, Marty would get a pair of shoes. Or a new jacket. Or a foot massage.

He had been going on shopping sprees all over town. Some days he was playing the part of Mr. Davidson. Other days he was Mr. Grace. Last Thursday he was Mrs. Frost. Then, he was #1749168—that's his jail ID number. When the police showed up at his house, Marty was actually wearing the Air Jordans he bought with Mrs. Frost's American Express. Brain freeze or brain fart?

"When it comes to theft, states have different amounts or limits on how much is stolen in determining if someone is charged with a misdemeanor versus a felony. Some make it over $300, some make it under. The penalties for using someone else's credit card without their permission also vary. The more you charge, the bigger the punishment. It's his first offense, so there's a strong chance he's not going to jail . . . but Marty's legal troubles are far from over.

"Stealing is obviously never acceptable. However, courts tend to be even stricter with people who take from their employers or family members. Judges are very hard on offenders who violate fiduciary duties. Fiduciary means there's a special kind of relationship created between people where a higher standard of loyalty or honesty is demanded. Just like grandma doesn't think you'll steal her Xanax from the medicine cabinet, an employer doesn't expect you to

pocket money from them . . . or their customers. They trusted you enough to give you a job in the first place.

Remember, these days, there are cameras everywhere. That's how they caught Marty. They even had him on video at the store trying on the gym shoes. So before reaching in the register or stealing something, if you can't hear the *EHnt*, at least look up and say 'cheese.'"

Vroom Vroom, Wee Woo Wee Woo.

Rusty couldn't wait to drive. So he didn't wait. He and his two buddies snuck into the garage at night and "borrowed" his parents' car. For a fourteen year old, this kid could fly. They did doughnuts up and down their high school's front lawn. Then, off to White Castle for some sliders—then, onto the highway. That was where they first hear the *wee woo wee woo* sounds.

What's the difference between joy riding and stealing a car?

"Joyriding is taking a car without intending to keep it. In contrast, a person who steals a car doesn't intend to return it to its owner. Auto theft is obviously much more serious."

Can you go to jail for joyriding?

"You absolutely can, but if it's your first offense and there's no accident, you probably won't. Most likely, you'll get charged with a misdemeanor and could lose your license or not be able to get one until you're eighteen years old. With stealing a car, it's a felony and you can go to jail."

What if the car you're joying around in belongs to your parents and you get in an accident? Will the insurance company cover it?

"That's a tricky question. The insurance company could say since Rusty is not on the policy, they're not paying."

Then who's responsible to pay?

"Rusty better hope the sushi restaurant is hiring!"

Shut Your Mouth, Blanco!

Charles was born in 1999 at 12:01 a.m. on December 25. He was named after his dad's favorite author, Charles Dickens, who wrote *Oliver Twist*. Almost immediately after coming into the world, he became Charlie to everyone. Until seventh grade.

Even if he were to sleep on the sun, Charlie couldn't get a tan. He looked like a walking cloud. So much so that one day at recess while choosing up sides for dodgeball, one of the other kids yelled out, "We pick blanco!" In Spanish, *blanco* means white. The nickname stuck like glue.

Home from college for the summer, Blanco was stopped for some minor traffic violation. Keep in mind, we should all try to cooperate with the police.

However, Blanco took it to a whole other level. After giving the officer his license, insurance, and registration, before the officer even asked a question, Blanco told him he lied to his boss today about being sick, he stole twenty dollars from his roommate's wallet, and he was getting a D in physics. I could be wrong, but in a few seconds, I think he was about to admit to killing Abraham Lincoln.

Isn't it better to be honest?

"Honest, yes. Confessing to assassinating the sixteenth president, no."

So, what's your recommendation for Blanco?

"It's okay to cooperate and be respectful. But you don't have to give away the farm. In other words, less equals more. Under the US Constitution, you have rights. One is to not incriminate yourself and another is to not talk with the police without having your lawyer present. As we've already learned, in today's world, almost everything is recorded, including police stops and arrests. If you want to give your lawyer the best chance to defend you regardless of the charge, confessing to everything under the sun won't help them do that."

Any other thoughts for Blanco?

"Get a tutor to help you with physics, try not to lie anymore to your boss, and don't steal twenty dollars from your roommate—but if you do, call your lawyer first!"

Weebles Wobble but They Don't Fall Down.

Casey and Asia had been friends since sixth grade. They met in music class and have been hanging out ever since. One of their favorite things to do together was pranking. One night they had egging on the agenda. It didn't matter the target. Houses, mailboxes, cars. They had never been caught. Until that night.

They meant to hit the side of the church's wall. They swore they did. However, unexpected winds caused their throws to sail high and to the left. *Crash, bam, kablooey.* The beautiful stained-glass windows were blown out to bits and pieces. Even if God was napping, He heard.

The two were picked up and brought to the local police station. Unfortunately, the sergeant on duty made sure they made the early bus to court where the strictest judge in the county sat. Although they got a bond, they also endured a twenty-minute public reprimand about their behavior.

You might be wondering what the difference is between simple vandalism and criminal damage to property. Any thoughts, Dumbo?

"Vandalism involves damaging someone's property. Like spray painting, graffiti, tearing up someone's lawn, keying a car, egg throwing, breaking windows—girls, did you hear that last part?"

And criminal damage to property?

"Well, it's spray-painting graffiti, tearing up someone's lawn . . . "

Wait, isn't that the same thing?

"Sometimes the law doesn't makes sense. They sound very similar, kind of the same thing. Often, criminal damage to property involves more serious damage."

Can you be charged with a felony for vandalism?

"Now seems like a good time to introduce you to the wobbler."

The wobbler?

"There are certain crimes, like these two and some others, where you could be charged with either a misdemeanor or a felony. The specific facts and how the prosecutor for the state chooses to charge you helps with this decision. Like a teeter-totter, it could go either way. This is why we call this one the wobbler. So next time, before throwing the eggs, *take a few lessons from the pitching coach on your school's baseball team."*

Raven and River Sitting in a Tree

River loved Raven. He wanted the whole world to know. For now, he settled for the people in his zip code. Recently, the city redid the sidewalk on his block. The cement was still wet. River had an idea how to ask his boo to junior prom. With a stick he drew the following message into the wet cement:

River ♡s Raven. Prom?

He also included ✋ underneath, which is his street gang's hand sign.

The next day, Mrs. Rodriguez from the apartment on the floor below River's called the police. By that time, the cement had dried. River was charged with graffiti and criminal damage to government property. A felony. He was stuck in jail for a week because his dad couldn't pay the $300 bond to get him out. When he was finally released, his job at the diner was gone.

Some argue graffiti is actually art.

Should River have asked boo to prom by drawing in the cement?

Probably not.

Should he have included the gang sign?

Maybe not.

Should he have been charged with a felony?

Absolutely not.

Why was he then?

Any thoughts, Picasso?

"Because the sidewalk is owned by the city, which makes it government property, and it costs $740 to repair it, this amount makes the crime a felony. Next time, please just send her a text!"

Speaking of Texts . . .

Prom?Prom?Prom?Prom?Prom?
Prom?Prom?Prom?Prom?Prom?
Prom?Prom?Prom?

Prom?Prom?Prom?Prom?Prom
?Prom?Prom?Prom?Prom?Prom?
Prom?Prom?Prom?Prom?Prom?
Prom?Prom?Prom?Prom?
Prom?Prom?Prom?Prom?Prom?
Prom?Prom?Prom?

It's okay to like someone. It's also okay to ask them out on a date. Once. Twice. Three times. Not 147.

Just like kids, harassment comes in all different shapes and sizes. One hundred phone calls can be considered telephone harassment, but so can one text. It depends just how aggravating what you're saying or sending is. So before forwarding that obscene text to the girl in French class or posting the threatening message to that boy from biology on Facebook, assume every single person living in the state of Texas is seeing it. Try not to put a single word, thought, or photo out there you wouldn't want those 58,000,000 eyeballs seeing.

Cyber bullying laws are getting more and more serious every day. They're created to protect teenagers from teenagers. Even though you may not think what you're saying or sending is a big deal, under the law it could be seen as a big deal. In many states, if the victim you're harassing or threatening is seventeen years old or younger, you can be convicted of a felony.

So how do you know what's considered illegal harassment or unlawful threatening versus simple teasing or just being the class bully?

A good test is ask yourself this:

Would I want someone saying or doing this to my little sister or brother? If the answer is no, please don't say it.

Thumper's Momma

"When we were first introduced, I shared how I got my name from the famous flying elephant in the Disney movie. Well, the message in this chapter comes from another Disney classic about a young deer named Bambi. In that

story, Thumper, a rabbit and friend of Bambi's, is scolded by his momma after he makes an unkind remark about his new friend. She tells him, 'If you don't have something nice to say, don't say anything at all.' Easier said than done, right? We all gossip. We all talk sh!t. We all say rotten things about each other we wish we could take back. Sometimes, we don't mean to be so mean. Other times, we actually do. The First Amendment of the US Constitution gives us freedom of speech to say almost anything we want. As we've already seen many times throughout this book, however, what we do (and say) during our yesterdays can unfortunately affect our tomorrows."

They created the acronym back in grammar school. Originally calling themselves the WAFFLES, because every Saturday morning they ate the same thing for breakfast together. Shortly thereafter, the word's trimmed down to just WAF—We Are Family. They met back in kindergarten. There were eight of them, and they all lived within a three-block radius of each other. Four girls, four boys. None of them were related, but they were closer than most sisters and brothers. With the exception of a few summer vacations, they spent nearly 365 days a year together for over a decade.

The original cause of their falls began at the start of eighth grade. Nobody is exactly sure who sent the first text. It doesn't really matter, though, because over that semester there were hundreds of messages flying back and forth between all the WAFs.

Like a carton of milk left in the back of the fridge for a week past its expiration date, the content of these texts were rotten. There is no reason to repeat the exact specifics. They may have learned their ABCs in preschool, but as young adults, let's just say it seems that their favorite letter was N. Think bad, then go deeper.

Racist, inflaming, infuriating, and sad. For the record, they were all pretty good kids from loving families. Those kinds of words weren't used at the dinner table. What is in your heart isn't always what comes through your thumbs. In other words, we aren't always what we text. And yet, once we hit Send, sometimes it's forever.

The WAFs went onto high school together and did great things academically, in sports, drama, music, and more. None of them had even one detention, not even a tardy. Close your eyes and choose the top colleges in the country—that's where each one got accepted. Until . . .

Years later, a group of other students discovered the disturbing texts and forwarded them to each university demanding accountability. Five of the eight WAFs got their university acceptances rescinded. The other three were under investigation.

"When we first met, I promised I would never lecture or try to frighten you with any of our stories. I guess I am a fibber. Because this particular topic warrants a lecture. Even though some could argue the WAFs may have naively sent these messages, their actions are coming back to haunt them."

You might be thinking this is unfair because they weren't even in high school yet. Shouldn't that be a defense? Dumbo?

"Not in today's society. There's no room for racism. If we're not moving forward together, we're simply drifting further apart."

What about the First Amendment and all that freedom of speech stuff?

"Remember we talked about how confusing and hazy today's marijuana laws are? Well, sometimes parts of the Constitution are equally as cloudy. The First Amendment gives us the right to say almost anything we want. Almost anything. There are exceptions, like child pornography, lying under oath in court, obscenity, blackmailing, or threatening to physically harm someone . . . and hate crimes. Under the law, in certain circumstances, racism, sexism, and other gender-related statements can be seen as hate crimes. Therefore, they are not protected by the Constitution."

Not to be a troublemaker, but taking back acceptances or kicking them out of school seems kind of harsh. Can't they ask for some kind of hearing or appeal?

"They can. And each college has the right to do whatever they determine is best for their schools and students. According to history, before becoming president, Abraham Lincoln said, 'And this, too, shall pass.' The WAFs will hopefully all go on to live happy and successful lives. However, make no mistake, those text messages will in some way always be linked to them.

"Living inside an overflowing volcano running a billion degrees at all times is not easy. Please don't make it harder for yourselves. Before pressing Send, hear the EHnt. Smell the rotten milk. See the 58,000,000 eyes reading what you wrote. Taste the tone of the words coming from your mouths. And *feel your futures being affected before they even have the chance to begin."*

My Thing Is Bigger Than Your Thing

Nicola was a great guy. Ask anyone. From his professors to his friends to the cashier at the campus coffee shop where he bought the same breakfast treat each morning before class. Everybody loved Nicola.

One Friday night, Nicola, his girlfriend, and his roommate went to Rocky's, a karaoke bar on Third Street. Although he had a daily ritual of eating chocolate doughnuts with sprinkles, Nicola also lifted weights six times a week. While waiting in line, a much smaller dude wearing a tank top and wrestling shoes started picking on Nicola's roommate. This guy was calling his roommate gay, rubbing his shoulders, and blowing in his ear. After a while, Nicola turned around and nicely asked him to quit it. The guy pushed Nicola in the chest, called him a f****t, and made some silly remark about the size of his penis.

Uh oh.

Nicola punched the guy and unfortunately broke his nose. The police came and Nicola got arrested. He was charged with battery and spent the night in jail.

What the heck. Tank Top Guy starts the whole thing. Anyone have a rational explanation?

"First, what a great name for a bar. I love karaoke."

Good to know. What do you think about Nicola?

"I think he's got a helluva right hook. Nice shot, champ."

What do you think about him getting locked up?

"I don't know Nicola, but what a class act standing up for his buddy; I get it. But you can't go around slugging guys wearing wrestling shoes in a bar. Especially ones just looking for trouble. You're going to run into a thousand of these kinds of people throughout your life. I know sometimes it's going to be hard—but you have got to walk away."

What about a self-defense argument and how he was standing up for his friend and all?

"First, remember in second grade when you first heard 'sticks and stones . . . ' Second, the law of self-defense is really complicated. You cannot use excessive force when defending yourself or others. It has to be reasonable, which is a term with many different interpretations. In other words, if I slug you in the arm, you can't hit me over the head with a hammer. It looks real cool in the movies when the good guy beats the sh!t out of the bad guy. In real life, it's just not worth it. If you find yourself in a situation where walking away is an option, walk tall."

Ronny Road Rage

Ronny recently got fired from the summer job he has had for the last three years. He had been saving up for a motorcycle. Not just any motorcycle, a Ducati, the Ferrari of motorcycles. He had already bought the helmet, which hung in his closet next to his leather biker jacket. Most nights you could find him wearing both in bed reading racing magazines.

As he drove home to break the news to his parents, he accidentally cut in front of another car. He quickly held up his hand in the rearview mirror signaling "sorry" to the other driver.

Man, Mom and Dad are gonna be really pissed off about me losing this job, he thought.

He turned onto the ramp to enter the highway. So did the BMW that was still traveling behind him. The guy was riding close enough to tell what month Ronny's license plate registration sticker expired in. He kept flashing his headlights on and off, on and off. Yelling out of his window. There it was, two birds at once—the old double middle-finger sign. Beemer Boy was obviously not happy about Ronny cutting him off.

Suddenly, the other car zoomed out of sight for a second, then it was right next to him with the driver launching F-bombs and screaming things about Ronny's mother that a son doesn't want to hear. He had saliva drooling down the corners of his mouth.

You know that feeling you get inside your chest when you first realize you're frightened? Ronny had it.

Ronny kept driving, looking straight ahead, trying not to pay attention, but this other guy wouldn't leave him alone. He demanded that Ronny pull over. *Where? I'm on the highway,* he thought to himself. He finally reached his exit and hit the turn signal.

So did the road-rager. Ronny was only a few miles from home, but there were six or seven stoplights on the way. At each one, the front fender of the BMW was kissing the back end of Ronny's Volkswagen. At Eastbrook Avenue, the other driver actually jumped out of his car and started walking toward the VW. Thankfully, the light turned green.

A few minutes later, the Beemer pulled into oncoming traffic and the driver glared right into Ronny's window.

Arrr, da knife, remember da knife! Ronny heard his dad's voice in his head.

Ronny remembered his father kept a knife in the glove compartment for when they go fishing and probably also just in case anyone in the family ever encountered a wacko operating a BMW. He quickly reached inside, grabbed the handle, and held it up against his window. The other driver's mouth opened wide like an exhausted hippo. He slammed on the gas pedal and off he went.

Phew, that was close.

An hour or so after Ronny got home, his mom yelled up for him to come downstairs. Standing in the foyer area were two uniformed police officers. Turns out, the other driver called 911 and reported how Ronny pulled a knife out and threatened him with it. While the taller officer put the handcuffs on Ronny, the other one shared how the driver who they interviewed at the station appeared to have pooped his pants.

Luckily, Ronny was only arrested for simple assault versus aggravated assault, which is usually the charge when a weapon is involved.

In the end, you'll be happy to hear Ronny's lawyer got the case thrown out of court. So what's the lesson here? What could each have done differently?

"Well, first to Beemer Boy. Shiver me timbers, matey. What are you thinking? This could've gone so much worse. You could have seriously injured Ronny, yourself, or someone else. There's simply no reason for such behavior. Keep your rage in a cage!"

What about Ronny?

"Besides accidentally cutting in front of the boy in a Beemer, he acted pretty properly. He immediately apologized and tried to keep his cool. Reaching for the knife was not such a gem of an idea. Pay attention to that feeling in your chest, though. When he realized the guy's behavior was abnormal, he should have immediately dialed 911. Although not always possible, driving directly to a police station or pulling into a busy parking lot or gas station where there are witnesses is also another option. Truth be told, Ronny was in a really difficult situation.

"I'll tell you what he did do right. Some mechanics specialize in fixing fancy cars like Ferraris and BMWs. You would never take one of these exotic beauties to a Volkswagen repairman, would you? No offense, VW lovers. It's the same

with lawyers. My cousin, Denny Dumbo, is a professional jewel thief. Remember, he's got eight arms! Whenever he gets arrested, he calls someone who specializes in getting the handcuffs off—same guy Ronny used. If you ever do need a lawyer, make sure you hire the right one."

Dream Weavers

According to mathematician and physicist Sir Isaac Newton, "every action in nature has an equal and opposite reaction." In other words, every choice we make carries certain consequences. On Sunday afternoon, Debbie unfortunately learned first hand just how right Sir Isaac was . . .

Her family owned *Dream Weavers* since before she could walk. Although small and over twenty years old, to Debbie and her siblings, the boat was a yacht. Together they had built a billion memories on it. It had been like their floating treehouse. The two words engraved on the back of the boat were inspired by Debbie's mom's favorite 1979 pop song—and coincidentally, Weaver is also their last name. Even as a third grader, Debbie always dreamed of someday being the captain. In high school, her parents finally loosened the knot and began letting her take friends out on the weekends. They had one rule. No alcohol.

There are moments in life when part of our brain whispers, *Please, dear God, can't we just go back to five seconds ago, before this all happened . . .* Oh, how Debbie wishes she could turn back the clock.

It was a sunny afternoon in late August, and Debbie and her four besties were out on *Dream Weavers*. Kat, one of her friends, invited two cousins who were visiting from out of town to join the crew. One of the brothers brought a twenty-four pack as a nice gesture for hosting them on the boat. They must have lost seven or eight white balls off the dock that day playing beer pong. Later, the Coast Guard would find a severed foot close by one of the balls, which must have drifted out to the middle of the lake where the accident occurred.

After hanging inside the harbor dancing and drinking for a few hours, Debbie decided to take the boat out for a spin. Cruising around the lake, she started making doughnuts, creating swirling waves. Suddenly, she lost control, and everyone was tossed into the water. However, the boat kept going on its own without anyone behind the wheel, spinning in a circle, striking three of the passengers, who were bobbing up and down. One of the cousins was struck by a propeller, cutting off his left foot right below the ankle. Kat was smashed by the front of the boat, instantly dislocating her shoulder. Another girl's chin was slit, requiring twenty-nine stitches. Thankfully it's a lake, not an ocean, so sharks aren't drawn by all the blood.

Debbie was charged with felony boating under the influence, lost her driver's license for a year, and faced the probability of going to jail. The injured parties filed civil lawsuits against Debbie and her mom and dad seeking damages against the Weavers in excess of $1 million. The boat was also seized by the state.

Land ho! Batten down the hatches, all hands on deck, and abandon ship. How could Debbie's parents possibly be charged criminally or sued civilly for a million dollars when they weren't even on the boat? Any help from someone who navigates in rough waters?

"Traditionally, parents will not be charged criminally for the crimes committed by their kids. However, let's say the Weavers are the ones who gave the kids the beer. Or they knew there was going to be drinking that day. Or even if they just left alcohol on the boat knowing Debbie and her friends were going on it, they could also be charged criminally with a felony. And face jail time."

O Captain, My Captain, that doesn't seem fair!

"The voyage of being a parent sometimes isn't fair. No alcohol means no alcohol. Never getting behind the wheel and driving means never—even if the 'vehicle' is a twenty-year-old boat. Remember, Zero Tolerance!"

Okay, what about this lawsuit. Mr. and Mrs. Weaver weren't driving the boat, they weren't on the boat, and didn't know some girl's out-of-town cousin was bringing beer. Can they still really have to pay a million bucks?

"Yep. They own the boat. They let their teenage daughter drive the boat. Her negligent actions transfer or attach to them."

Okay, but at least they have insurance to protect them, right?

"Not so fast. That's kind of a gray area. Some insurance companies will deny coverage if alcohol is involved. So, whether the accident is in a car, a boat, or on a bike, if the driver's drunk, the owners of *Dream Weavers* could have a really big nightmare."

What's the message here Captain Dumbo?

"Every choice carries consequences. Hearing the *EHnt* can not only protect you, but it can protect someone you love."

Before a Summer Storm

PJ and Sophie had been dating for almost fourteen months. They met in algebra class. PJ just made her the most creative Valentine's Day present out of old metal he found in his garage. PJ was also vice president of student council.

One day, they were in the high school bleachers arguing about how Sophie was flirting with Billy at the bowling alley last weekend. One thing led to another, and before she knew it, PJ had slugged her in the face. There was nobody else around, but it didn't matter. Sophie's left eye was already swollen and resembled the sky right before a big summer storm.

I have three questions I'd like your Honor to answer.

What if PJ was drunk? Would that be a defense for his behavior?

What if this was the very first time PJ ever hit Sophie, and he was really, really sorry—would that excuse his behavior?

What if Sophie didn't want PJ to get in trouble and refused to file charges, should that make the case go away?

"A man never hits a woman. And although females are also arrested for the offense, make no mistake—more often than not, males are charged with domestic battery. So for those boys who choose not to listen, know that the domestic battery law is tricky. If found guilty, you could go to jail, and you will definitely have a permanent criminal mark on your record following you around for life."

Anything else, judge?

"Yes. For those people who think it's okay for someone to hurt them because the other person happens to be drunk or because it only happens once or because the other person feels really, really bad about their behavior, here are three places to contact:"

The National Domestic Violence Hotline at 800-799-7233 or
Love is Respect at 866-331-9474 or
Email Dumbo at rshindler@sbcglobal.net.

Court is back in session:

"Okay, Arthur. Now that you've plead guilty and have been placed on probation, do you understand your responsibilities under your sentence?"

"Yes, your Honor, I do. And I want to thank you for giving me this opportunity. I've learned my lesson, and I promise I won't let you down."

"I hope not, because you should know the court does not take these charges lightly. You are eligible for this type of probation only because you do not have any prior criminal history. Please don't do anything to mess this up. Good luck to you, and don't forget to report to your probation officer before leaving the courthouse. Court is adjourned."

Arthur's name begins with the letter A. Do you know what else starts with an A? The word *amnesia*. Because just thirty-four days later, Arthur forgot the promise he made to the judge about not letting him down.

Arthur had been sentenced to probation for possession of cocaine. However, since it was his first arrest, he was eligible for 410 probation. In Illinois, this is a special kind of disposition available only to first-time felony drug offenders. It allowed Arthur to avoid a felony conviction going on his permanent record. It's a second chance. And the requirements to succeed are so easy to satisfy that even, well . . . even a mighty, tiny octopus could do it.

Unfortunately, Art's no octopus. Besides not getting caught with a weapon, paying a small fine, finishing high school, and performing thirty hours of public service, the only other requirement is to not test positive for drugs. I guess Arthur missed the memo on that last one.

The following weekend, Art's school held their homecoming dance. After the dance, Arthur did a few lines of coke at a party. The next day, he was scheduled to see Terrence, his probation officer, where he was required to take a random drug test. Art freaked out about potentially testing positive on the test, so he came up with a brilliant idea. His friend Victor didn't do drugs. So he had Vic pee in a vial for him, and he brought it in his coat pocket to the appointment. There was only one problem with his master plan. There was a hole in his pocket.

As he and his probation officer walked to the bathroom together—*plop, plop!* The vial fell out of his pocket, broke on the floor, and sprayed urine all over the bottom of poor Terrence's suit pants. Terrence was not a happy camper. After being required to pee in a cup himself, not only was Arthur charged with violating the terms of his probation for testing positive for cocaine, he was also arrested and charged with a brand-new felony:

Attempt to defraud a drug screening test, which is a class 4 felony punishable by one to three years in jail.

Hey Dumbo, any droplets of wisdom for us—what's the moral of the story?

"Listen, we all make mistakes. The trick is, whenever you do, don't do anything to make the problem worse. And when

we're given a second chance by our parents, teachers, friends,
or a judge, don't number two (or number one) on it!

"Th-th-th-that's all folks!"

CONCLUSION

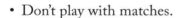

Rules, Rules, and More Rules

- Don't play with matches.
- Don't talk to strangers.
- Say please and thank you.
- Always wear clean underwear.

As I said in the very beginning, in my opinion, you have it way harder than any other generation before you. The world is watching from sun up to sun down. Let's be honest. You're probably gonna play with matches. You're going to talk to strangers. And occasionally, you'll even forget to change your underwear. That's not what worries the people who love you. It's the dangerous potholes you face during your journey into adulthood. The turns taken that can lead you into dark alleys. Those are the ones keeping us up at night.

"Stay in your lane" is a phrase traditionally meaning MYOB—mind your own business. Please know my intention was never to tell you what to do; it was more me trying to guide you on what not to do. Hopefully I've provided just a little bit of knowledge that you can keep in your back pocket just in case you ever need it on a rainy day.

I wish you what I wish my kids. Choices.

"You're braver than you believe, stronger than you seem, and smarter than you think."

A. A. Milne

Have a Great Life!

Acknowledgments

To my parents up in Heaven and my parents on Ravine Drive.

To Keith and Derv, you were my very first roommates, and I loved growing up with both of you by my side.

To Marc, Adam, Rick, JP, Rusty, and Jeff, you kept me safe, taught me how to laugh, and even when I only weighed 70 pounds, you made me feel like a superhero.

To everyone at Mascot Books, especially Rebecca, Joe, Matt, Hobbs, and, of course, Dr. Nicole, who started as my project manager, but finished as my therapist and friend.

To every lawyer I have worked with and every judge I've stood before, it has been a pleasure being part of the same noble profession together.

To my clients, who give me a chance to give them a chance.

And to Alma, who brings sunshine, hope, and integrity to me each and every day. You truly are and forever will be my SFAM.

About the Author

For more than three decades, Rob has been in private practice representing generations of families facing life-altering legal problems. He and his wife Andi, also a lawyer, live in Chicago and have raised three amazing children: Isabella, Oliver, and Sage. Fairy tales really do come true.